The Battle of the Sexes

A New Perspective on a Lost Religion

By Robert Villegas

The Battle of the Sexes – A New Perspective on a Lost
Religion
By
Robert Villegas

Robertv1989@outlook.com

ISBN-13: 978-1519147172
ISBN-10: 1519147171
Library of Congress Control Number 2016903362
Series Title: Villegas Religion

Published in the United States of America

Social Media Addresses

Parler: @Robertv1989

CloutHub @RobertVillegas

MeWe Robert Villegas

Minds @Robertv1989

Gab @V4Vendata

Dedicated to my Aphrodite

Table of Contents

Introduction

In my book, Behind the Ritual Mask, I introduced the concept of cultural role paradigms and identified three basic paradigms that were created by religion. In that book, I pointed out that these cultural role paradigms displace reason as the methods for defining action. As a result of these paradigms and their imposition by religious institutions and government, mankind has been led down the road of altruism, collectivism and the good/evil split which desecrate the value of the individual and his life. In my research for this book, I learned about a fourth, equally important, cultural paradigm that represented a lost religion as distinguished from those that have come down to us. This religion, although buried in pre-history, is still being practiced today as an underground cultural paradigm. It is called The Battle of the Sexes.

How is it that people can practice a religion and not know it? They do it by suspending reason and engaging in ritual activities that have lost their connection to their sources in pre-history. We get a glimpse of the religion when we analyze patterns and themes in the available literature. From this literature, we can learn what the original events or stories have come to mean in modern times and through effective analysis identify their philosophical premises.

A cultural role paradigm is a replacement for morality. It is an example from mythology that developed during man's pre-reason periods that functioned as morality then and became a role model later. Believing individuals integrate these role paradigms into their lives by consciously or subconsciously emulating the actions of the gods throughout their lives. Each paradigm represents a role that is assigned to people by culture, religion or religiously influenced people.

As we will see, the Battle of the Sexes role paradigms include three separate roles that have come down to modern man virtually intact. They are Aphrodite, Ares and the male version of Venus known as Hephaistos.

Hephaistos, as the husband of Aphrodite is considered to be the victim who was cuckolded by her when he was forced to watch her engage in a sexual encounter with the god Ares. In literature, one of the first instances of reenactment of this event was the relationship between Helen of Troy, Paris and Menelaus, her cuckolded husband. This event was not only enacted in the story but was also told as a festival performance in Homer's Odyssey. As we will see, this theme made up the fundamental conflict of the Iliad.

Some would call these characters "archetypes" that have come to represent fundamental role types that influence morality and culture. Aphrodite is the beautiful seductress who cavalierly dismisses her husband in favor of the powerful, strong and handsome lover who enters her domain for the purpose of sexual conquest. Hephaistos is the lame cuckold who must perennially distrust his wife, who not only watches her infidelity from afar but is also intelligent enough to turn the tables on the lovers and catch them in the act, holding them hostage and demanding payment.

Inevitably, man bases his religions, his primitive philosophical systems, upon role characters such as these three. He bases them, ultimately, on connections he finds in his own life. God takes the form of a father and he tells himself that God created man in his own image. The Gods war against each other and he tells himself that God has ordered him to make war. A man makes love to a woman and he tells himself that Ares made love to Aphrodite. A man worships beauty in a woman, finds love and innocence in her example and looks up into the sky to worship the shining ethereal Venus. Everywhere we see the connection between what is taken to be the life of the gods and the life of man as he struggled through the Neolithic period and today.

The religion derived from the myth of the Battle of the Sexes became connected to man's common method of building relationships with others, and in particular his sexual practices and standards of beauty. As above, so below; or rather, as below, so above.

The Battle of the Sexes

We must not underestimate the power of religion (any religion) to inform morality. The sources of many religious concepts were the developing cultures of the prehistoric periods; and although morality today grew out of an amalgamation of early religious concepts, their purpose was to insinuate a moral base and influence the actions of posterity into infinity (as long as the culture lasted).

Man is a creature of a certain sort, he has a mind and a body both of which are natural elements. If used in a certain way, these natural elements influence what man becomes. Over several millennia, natural selection emphasized human qualities that led to survival and it was those individuals who procreated the most who survived. The human mind, over these millennia, became more competent and the human body became more capable as man learned to use them to accomplish survival.

Major developments in human societies were an outgrowth of man's intellectual capabilities as well as his physical capabilities. These developments not only improved man's ability to survive, they did so with exponentially beneficial results. These developments included language, agriculture, fire, food processing, the wheel and written communication which improved the developing mind. They helped make man the dominant creature on the planet.

Notice that I did not mention religion as one of these developments. Certainly, religion was a child of man's developing nature, but not one of the developments that spurred a major advance. Religion is actually "pre-philosophy", a sort of subconscious effort to understand reality and the nature of the world. It could only assist the effort to advance man's survival once its major premises, an outgrowth of man's sensory mechanism and developing mind, were converted into explicit conceptual expressions that conformed to the real world. Once man developed the ability to make his knowledge conform to the real world, he could then advance to the philosophical level which could spur human development. We have barely started on that path, but the beginning was the effort to understand the elements of existence (water, fire, air, and earth) as opposed to the spiritual which led to religion.

This last premise was one of the key observations I made in my book, Behind the Ritual Mask. In this book, I identified three cultural paradigms that were an outgrowth of man's effort to understand the world and define principles that could influence both survival and flourishing. Pre-religious concepts, cultural role paradigms, were man's feeble attempt to understand "how things work". And because man had yet to develop the vocabulary necessary for advanced levels of abstraction (from his sensory input), religion could only inform through primitive descriptions of past events or stories. This led to the development of religion and the injunction for man to emulate the gods. The three most influential of these were collectivism (the chorus), the good/evil paradigm (spirit vs. body) and the suffering savior (human sacrifice). I showed in Behind the Ritual Mask how these implicit role paradigms served the purpose of providing examples for proper thought and action and I showed that these paradigms provided the foundation for what man "knows" and, as such, they provided a bulwark against the advance to higher philosophical development. In effect, because role paradigms are entrenched in subconscious thought patterns, heavily laden with emotion, they are our biggest obstacles to philosophical knowledge. They bring about much war, conflict and mass murder. They keep us from understanding and developing the proper intellectual foundations for proper society, proper morality and proper science because metaphysical terms are properly neutral emotionally. A role paradigm necessarily corrupts metaphysical thinking which should, at base, be neutral emotionally. This harms judgment and human psychology by creating fear of the ineffable and doubt.

Yet, in my previous book, I chose to leave out a particular set of role paradigms because I didn't consider them fundamental to the goal of my book. This cultural paradigm is called "the Battle of the Sexes".

I am convinced that this paradigm is highly influential and even interesting. It is still working in our culture, and is steeped in sexual roles and rituals that dominate human relationships around the world. Many people live their whole lives unaware that their relationship problems stem from this paradigm and nothing else. It creates tremendous confusion, misunderstanding, prejudice and strife. It ruins male/female relationships and destroys the ability of people to engage in reason in an area of their deepest and most important choices, i.e. their sexual lives. It creates self-doubt, fear and guilt, and is yet the most common trap into which human beings fall.

We are going to embark, in this book, into a new field that I call Psychological Archaeology. As we have discussed with the first three paradigms in my other book, we are going to look into the mind of ancient, pre-historical man, by analyzing his mythology, to see if we can understand the roots of the modern world.

This is a daunting task and one riddled with many difficult questions. Yet, I believe this analysis will yield some significant new understandings of just how "religious" our society is and how ancient ideas are still doing psychological harm today. The new concepts brought forward here will open up new windows of understanding about man, his past and how ideas in the past became what they are today.

I will repeat here what I have written previously about ancient cultural paradigms:

"Ancient cultural paradigms are ideas or examples that developed as a consequence of man's efforts to interpret the meanings of specific pre-historical events. In the past, man may have sought to understand major events in pre-history by developing stories and myths that enabled him to pass information to his progeny. Through ancient cultural paradigms, man became an emulator of the gods, doing what the gods did in order to integrate the identity and characteristics of the gods into his own personality. He used examples from his own life and survival methods in order to explain or communicate the meaning of these events and to give them moral import. Many of these original ideas have been reinterpreted over time and the sources of those ideas have been lost. Yet, today these ideas provide our material culture and traditional foundations. We wear our cultural premises on our bodies and they form much of our outward expressions, clothing, jewelry, art, music, etc.

"And yet, we can learn something about cultural paradigms through archaeology, psychology, analysis of ancient texts and through objective religious studies. Out of early man's relationship with father came god; out of that with mother came the virgin mother or Venus; out of that with animals in the hunt came the animal deities; out of man's struggle to survive came the struggle of the gods against each other; out of his tools of survival came the tools and weapons of the gods, etc.

"An action taken by what was interpreted to be a god may have been converted allegorically into a moral premise in order to create understanding and import for man and his life as it was. Eventually, these allegories became stories about the gods converted to ritual reenactments, then rituals, then religious morality. The gods may have actually been the planets and an interpretation of the movements of those planets through the skies may have been the actions of the gods. I don't think that it was a coincidence that the names of the planets were also the names of many of the gods.

"Nevertheless, somewhere in prehistory, man interpreted global or cosmic events as expressions of traditional relationships and created powerful moral messages that have been embedded in culture. These messages were originally told as stories of the lives of the gods and became expressions, with the gods as paradigms of what man already knew as his life; he interpreted his own life by reference to these examples and invented religious culture as foundation for future generations. Material culture became, over centuries, a photograph-like expression, a memory preserved in art. Material culture expressed the metaphysical make-up of the world as understood by this emerging creature and the societies that he developed.

"Each role paradigm (or example) has a prototype or source that is most often lost in the unwritten-about past and is expressed, for the most part, through ancient religious themes and modern moral lessons. The modern manifestation of a cultural paradigm is a subconscious set of morals and actions that are seen as imperatives (rituals) by a large number of people (i.e., Jesus as paradigm) and social institutions. Somewhere in the past, man was instructed by cultural leaders to perform "rituals," repetitive acts that achieved a number of social goals. These rituals were reenactments of those early events in the lives of the gods and provided a sort of social cohesion and expression, catharsis.

"Early rituals became the mystery religions. The mystery religions became drama, sport, theater and art. These became morality when man was exhorted to act out in daily living all the things the gods did in order to be like the gods, propitiate the gods and gain their favor.

"Today's cultural paradigms are based upon the experience of the culture and develop within both society and the individual into conscious and subconscious thought patterns that function as knowledge when in fact, today, they are not knowledge but allegories disconnected intellectually from their sources in reality. As such they form the foundation for the values of the culture and of individuals, providing support for individual decisions. Most importantly, when they form, through rationalism, the foundation for generally accepted knowledge, they replace the normal role of reason in decision-making. Their most profound impact is in the every-day decisions and judgments made by individuals and institutions. Since those decisions are founded in collectivism (the chorus), self-sacrifice (the suffering savior) and prejudice against man (moral dualism), mankind has inadvertently embedded the negative consequences of these cultural influences into his actions and life.

"Our culture has a submerged, or subconscious, source of knowledge that comes from pre-history. Some information is known about it because of the mystery religions that dominated the world prior to Christianity's dominance and from Greek plays and other mythologies. Indeed, much of Christianity has incorporated the fundamental paradigms found in the mystery religions, especially the Suffering Savior, Good/Evil and Chorus paradigms…"[1]

In the next chapter, we will examine the second set of cultural paradigm that I have selected for study called the Battle of the Sexes. This paradigm has created three roles for man to play in his daily living and has laid the foundation for attitudes and behaviors that are based in acceptance of ritualized roles rather than reason. As we will see, the Battle of the Sexes is

[1] Behind the Ritual Mask

not simply a matter of sexual humor and man/woman relationships. It is a fully *religious* paradigm that is replete with ritual and religious premises. It is derived from one of our most enduring and powerful myths.

When the When was the What

"Teacher: Consider, child! From whom do these gifts come? You can have nothing from yourself.
Child: Oh!, I got it all from Daddy.
Teacher: And he? where did he get it from?
Child: From Grandpapa.
Teacher: No, no! How did it all come to Grandpapa then?
Child: He took it."[2]

Ancient stories and myths developed out of a need for reflection on the meanings of events ancient man considered worth remembering. The timing of the event became not only the when but also the what, a generalized reference point that stayed in the memory of men for generations and even centuries. Throughout early times, these stories were told and retold because it was pleasurable to hear them, they held special meanings that men wanted to give to their offspring. They sought to understand their meanings and use them as guides for the future.

Before we get too far into our discussion, I'd like to point out that I don't ascribe to the idea of a collective consciousness. I don't think that knowledge or memories are handed down to men by any means other than direct communication between individuals. I think man's mind is tabula rasa, each individual is born essentially with a blank slate and there is no imprinting upon it made by previous generations

---

[2] Goethe, Selected Verses

except that which is imprinted by the tales and stories that the individual is told by others. For instance, I don't think that there is a memory implanted in us as a group or even as individuals. When we are born we don't know anything about Jesus or Ares or Aphrodite even as vague essences. We either accept what we are told or we question it. Knowledge is not passed down collectively.

The ideas presented to us as individuals come down to us as memories because they were communicated from generation to generation or written down at some point from oral traditions. This is why many men are constantly referring to scriptures when they discuss religion. There is absolutely no evidence for the existence of a collective consciousness as there is no evidence for an Absolute Mind, angels or communication with the dead.

With that said, it is important that we understand that primordial icons, arch-types and symbols as they were passed down to us verbally, helped commemorate past events with their meanings embedded, by implication, in symbols. Indeed, there were several types of stories told: tales of the hunt and success, stories of dire catastrophe and stories of the gods and the events of their lives – including their relationships with man, were all told over and over, generation to generation, and eventually passed down to us as "morality plays" and social institutions.

Surprisingly, the stories of the gods were told from the context of the knowledge available to early men at the time when they began to be remembered. This is why many of them include animal spirits, the implements of warfare and Neolithic agricultural lifestyles. Eventually, the stories became what we know to be our ancient myths. The "when" became the "what" but was expressed in terms of the intellectual context of the story teller who may have been several generations removed from the original event. When "god" intervened in a war, for instance, the nature of that "god" may not have been communicated correctly by the first story tellers and today that god seems ineffable and mysterious. The story tellers were trying to describe what the god did but he was not scientifically capable of understanding it himself. What they meant to describe may have been something we can understand scientifically today or something that we would be able to easily identify with our more extensive knowledge of nature and our more advanced vocabulary. The ancients were not so lucky in that regard.

Early literature (mythology) and even modern literature have the added psychological benefit of helping man connect with and express his deepest "hidden" issues, fears and trauma. Through literature, man can relive and "experience" the feelings of other men involved in the stories and he can relate them to his own situation and feelings. Any fear he has may be sublimated and subconsciously converted into a ritual reenactment of much less intensity than the original trauma. This helps him deal with his doubts and fears by reducing their magnitude psychologically.

An early story teller would have used body language, facial expressions, and voice inflection to craft a tale that had depth and meaning. These expressions would have kept his listeners "on the edge of their seats" while they waited to learn if the heroes accomplished their tasks. These early story tellers were also revered as men of deep knowledge and moral understanding. They imparted moral messages about how man should live, as it was expressed to them by the "gods." Eventually, men decided that retelling a story was not good enough…why not reenact the story and allow men to watch, hence the birth of mystery religions, morality plays and eventually theater and movies. Few people realize that many movies we see today are retellings of ancient myths.

I have long believed that going to a movie has the same psychological benefit as going to church. In each activity, the individual is allowed to watch the same story, the suffering savior, reenacted over and over; he is allowed to relive and enjoy the life of this hero who grapples with nearly insurmountable odds to save humanity through his bravery. The stories are the same as the rituals and the rituals are the same as the myths and the myths are the same as the petroglyphs that were pointed to while the fire raged in a cave with men, women and children sitting there enthralled. The smiles and laughter and wonderment and emotions in the audience are the same. Find a director who knows that there are only three basic stories to tell and you have a successful director who knows how to craft a story: they are, the suffering savior myth and the battle of the sexes myth and the success of the hunt story. There are no other stories (at least not yet), just variations on a theme.

Why is this so? The suffering savior story is about morality, saving people, helping men and encouraging action that affects society; the battle of the sexes story is about love, male/female relationships, happiness and even laughter; the success in the hunt story is about survival and conflict with nature. How can you be more basic than that? Today, man is still a hunter, a lover and a hero.

To a great extent, literature grew out of the time measured by mathematics…not directly of course, but over time, perhaps over millennia. Mathematics was originally a tool used for measuring time that was then converted to the practice of counting. Time was a way of connecting the "what" (event) with the "when." For man, the extreme importance of understanding events contained the contextual question of when those events took place. In order to measure himself and his activities, his accomplishments and his inventions, man had to be able to document when he did what or when he saw what or what happened when. This was crucial for a creature who wanted to understand the past in order to build upon his understanding and gain a better knowledge to carry forward. The result of the successful story was catharsis, understanding and social cohesion. Hence the first intellectual creation (the first stories) of man must have been about "when" "what" happened.

But when the "what" *was* the "when" (i.e. the original

event) you had primitive knowledge and primitive language which is one of the reasons we have difficulty deciphering many ancient scripts. Men divided time by means of the ages – the start of which was both a "when" and a "what." You aren't going to tell an enduring story about yesterday's breakfast; you want something important, monumental, something that inaugurated a new age, heroic acts that set the foundation for teaching man how he should act. Only those kinds of stories could bring catharsis, understanding and inspiration – this was the birth of entertainment as well as morality.

Another example of how the "when" becomes the "what" is found in our sports. Notice that many sports utilize a ball that must somehow be moved toward a goal which results in points being scored by one team over the other. This activity is a reenactment of something in mythology, a sort of battle of the gods, and represents a particular event that at one time meant something important for men (and that they chose to reenact ritually through sport). It is myth becoming sport (which is a reenactment of a war), a when becoming a what that is important for men, reflects their values, two of which are heroism and accomplishment. Spectators and participants reach cathartic release when they watch and enjoy the victory of their team and they become despondent when their team loses. A good example is the pleasure the Phaecians in the Odyssey expressed when they watched the new sport of pitch and catch of the red ball in the Odyssey. They marveled in wonderment at the ball flying through the air and admire the athlete who is nimble enough to catch it and throw it back. Their reaction is a remembrance of something that yields catharsis. That they marveled while we today take it for granted indicates that it was something that happened within their memory.

To understand this more fully, I have developed the following hypothetical chronology to explain how man could have moved from image to concept to idea:

1. An event of significant meaning occurs ("what" and "when" are synonymous and known).
2. In order to remember the event, an image or pictograph (or petroglyph) was developed that records what primitive man saw when the event occurred – this is an ancient photograph – this is the "what" but we are losing the "when" after time and generations pass. We have then only the pictograph as a vague memory and seeing the image indicates that something spectacular happened that is worthy of remembrance.
3. The glyph is then used as the foundation for telling a story that commemorates the original event but is explained in terms familiar to man, for instance, a shooting star may be described as an eagle that flies in the sky or a god fallen to earth – the when and the what are becoming a story but also something men can emulate and do. This is because man loves greatness and spectacular feats and wants to emulate the gods.
4. An effort to understand the meaning of the event is undertaken and an allegory (myth) is developed (the "what" is remembered within the

context of the level of knowledge of primitive man, the when is lost over time). All we know is that it was long ago and foundational.

5. The myth becomes an allegory for life, the actor is either a "god" or ancestor with each man becoming the "actor" in the myth and gaining a new moral understanding for his own use (religious ethics is born).

6. From allegory, a reenactment (ritual) takes place that becomes embedded in the culture as common action and expression (retellings) of the myth that yield moral understanding as opposed to the original metaphysical understanding (myth becomes allegory). The ritual takes on prescribed activities that must be repeated regularly in order to enable man to "remember" the original story and extract meaning from it.

7. Men engage in rites in order to better understand subconsciously the meaning of the original event and in order to commemorate the role and importance of the "gods" or ancestors in their lives (mystery rites and Greek drama are born).

8. The principle of progressive benignity[3] and sublimation work to minimize the cruel aspects of the original ritual in the hope that the "gods" or ancestors will be propitiated by a reenactment in real life engaged by men as moral imperatives – the ritual of human

---

[3] See my book Behind the Ritual Mask.Progressive benignity is the reduction of trauma from early prehistorical events that lessen the demands of the gods by turning them into more benign expressions such as human sacrifice over time becoming contributing to charity.

sacrifice becomes sacrificing a bull or contributing money to the temple, being kind to others and loving your neighbor.

9. Religious morality becomes ritual reenactment masquerading as proper action prescribed by what is now a benign god and/or his earthly representative – a schizophrenic who speaks to god (the principle of progressive benignity has affected our definition of god – god is no longer something real and visible but something ethereal and mysterious).

10.   Men play role paradigms prescribed by ritual reenactments in their everyday lives without choice or challenge and suffer the same psychological problems that gave rise to the original interpretation of the significant event – the psychology is embedded in the role paradigm but interpreted differently within the present social context.

11.   Cultural paradigms are passed from generation to generation with the subconscious minds of generations of men as the conduit – men subconsciously perform rituals and roles that they think they are required to perform lest they obtain the ire of society, society's leaders or God. Reason is destroyed and the paradigm becomes ethical action prescribed by God. Men repeat mindlessly the ritual of self-sacrifice. The when has now become the what. The past informs the present and men perform the roles of the gods in their everyday lives without knowing they are being "religious".

The surprise comes when we realize that what has

been lost from prehistory may not be as much as we have thought. The stories found in our myths may actually be represented by certain iconic images or petroglyphs and these can give us an opportunity to learn more about what primitive man experienced and thought in a moral sense. The original events may be embedded in the icons and as a consequence we may be able to identify which icons represent which events and, through detective work and psychological analysis, we may be able to identify the time when the events occurred.
We also have archaeology to aid us because it uncovers many artifacts that give us clues about when certain images became prominent.
Archaeology also enables us to understand the record of destruction of many ancient sites as well and how they were destroyed.

To illustrate one such story we will examine the story of Helen of Troy because it is the most vivid expression of the story of the Battle of the Sexes.

The Trojan War

A young prince named Paris visits Sparta, the city of
a Greek king named Menelaus, where he is treated
with respect and courtesy. Paris is enchanted by the
magnificent beauty and seductive powers of
Menelaus' wife, Helen. After Paris seduces her, he
convinces her to leave with him for his home Troy.
With this "escape" by Helen, the foundation for the
story is laid and the Trojan War is the result. But
Paris's kidnapping of Helen and the subsequent
anger of Menelaus becomes a monumental theme for
a story that reflects a fundamental paradigm that has
significantly influenced our own time. It is the
skeleton of our modern Battle of the Sexes.

Paris, who would later be the kidnapper of Helen of
Troy, has an interesting history. When he was born, a
seer predicted that he would bring about the
destruction of Troy. The remedy was that he be killed
in infancy. His mother and father struggled with the
decision to kill their son and neither of them was able
to do the deed. In a story reminiscent of the Oedipus
story, King Priam, the boy's father, turned the boy
over to his herdsman to take him into the wilderness
to do the deed. Ala Oedipus, the herdsman could not
kill the boy with his own hand and left him to die in
the desert whereupon the boy was suckled by a she-
bear and he was later found by the herdsman alive.
At this point, the herdsman decided to raise the boy
himself and cut out the tongue of an animal to "prove"
to King Priam that the boy had been killed.

Paris's connection to the god Ares was established while he was still a young boy breeding fighting bulls (the bull is a personification of Ares). He was so successful at breeding great bulls that Ares decided to come to earth as a bull and compete with one of Paris's bulls. Of course, Ares was successful against Paris's bull which established a connection for Paris as a favorite of Ares.

Paris's connection to Aphrodite (the goddess who is the equivalent of Helen) was also established when he was young. He was asked to judge a contest between Aphrodite, (presumably the moon) Hera (earth) and Athena (Venus). He was bribed by Aphrodite with a promise of the most beautiful woman in the world should he choose her as the winner of the contest. After having done so, he earned the right to Helen but was not told that she was already married. His later abduction of Helen caused the Trojan War and Aphrodite served as his protectress during hand-to-hand combat with Menelaus (Hephaistos/Venus) over Helen.

But there is more to the story. Before the intrigue that accompanied the Battle of the Sexes cultural paradigm there is another more fundamental story which sets the grounds for the story of Paris and Helen. In fact, it represents a companion story that involves the gods.

As we will see, the Battle of the Sexes is, in my view, a psychologically deadly one because it establishes the cultural and psychological foundation for a profound alienation in man that has to do, not only with gender roles, but with a profoundly foundational principle that led to social movements based upon gender. Today, the love triangle is part of our ritualized foundation for both love stories and comedies about relationships (as well as for actual relationships). That it once had religious significance of profound meaning for man is hardly known to us. We see glimpses of it in the art of the Etruscans, Greeks, Romans and European medieval periods as well as the Renaissance.

Needless to say, Paris was a romantic and highly sexual man who fell deeply in love with Helen, so much in love that he was moved by his passion to kidnap her and bring her to his home inside the walled city of Troy. It is assumed that the kidnapping of Helen was more of an escape for her as she was also deeply attracted to Paris. It is likely that she was mere chattel to the brutish Menelaus, who, along with his brother Agamemnon, was probably bristling for a war anyway. Perhaps Menelaus was a devoted lover and a wonderful husband who was in love with the beauty, but that is not likely. Indeed, it is possible that his possession of Helen was based upon a previous kidnapping of his own.

Certainly, the idea of having another man whisk one's wife away is a hard pill for any man to swallow, especially if she *wants* to be whisked away. The key to understanding this story, however, is in the psychology of these three characters, what they represented in ancient religion and how their actions influenced people who heard the story.

Menelaus, in alliance with many other Argive warriors, in particular his ill-fated brother Agamemnon, launched their thousand ships and besieged the walled city of Troy for many years, sacrificed many lives, even had the gods involved in the conflict and, through the cunning of Odysseus, a brilliant Greek nobleman, eventually took the city, destroyed the Trojans and "rescued" the suddenly remorseful Helen from her ravaged lover. Helen is reunited with her husband and takes her rightful role as the queen of Menelaus' subjects, spending her time in the womanly ritual of spinning thread in emulation of her patron goddess, Aphrodite.[4]

---

[4] See the Iliad by Homer

The Real Story

There is an earlier story upon which the story of Helen and Paris is based. This story is called the Song of Love and the same poet (Homer) that told the story of the Trojan War has also provided.

Let us turn to the Odyssey by Homer which is the tale of how Odysseus was able to return to his home after the Trojan War. At this point in the story, the hero Odysseus has landed on a peaceful island called Phaecia where the people treat him with courtesy and respect. He is treated to a lavish dinner and entertainment by a blind bard named Demodocus. Demodocus sings the Love Song story while Phaecian dancers reenact it before Odysseus' eyes.

"Meanwhile the bard began to sing the loves of Ares and Aphrodite, and how they first began their intrigue in the house of Hephaestus. Ares made Aphrodite many presents, and defiled King Hephaestus' marriage bed, so the sun, who saw what they were about, told Hephaestus. Hephaestus was very angry when he heard such dreadful news, so he went to his smithy brooding mischief, got his great anvil into its place, and began to forge some chains which none could either unloose or break, so that they might stay there in that place. When he had finished his snare he went into his bedroom and festooned the bed-posts all over with chains like cobwebs; he also let many hang down from the great beam of the ceiling. Not even a god could see them, so fine and subtle were they. As soon as he had spread the chains all over the bed, he made as though he were setting out for the fair state of Lemnos, which of all places in the world was the one he was fondest of. But Ares kept no blind lookout, and as soon as he saw him start, hurried off to his house, burning with love for Aphrodite.

"Now Aphrodite was just come in from a visit to her father Zeus, and was about sitting down when Ares came inside the house, and said as he took her hand in his own, "Let us go to the couch of Hephaestus: he is not at home, but is gone off to Lemnos among the Sintians, whose speech is barbarous.

"She was nothing loath, so they went to the couch to take their rest, whereon they were caught in the toils which cunning Hephaestus had spread for them, and could neither get up nor stir hand or foot, but found too late that they were in a trap. Then Hephaestus came up to them, for he had turned back before reaching Lemnos, when his scout the sun told him what was going on. He was in a furious passion, and stood in the vestibule making a dreadful noise as he shouted to all the gods.

""Father Zeus," he cried, "and all you other blessed gods who live forever, come here and see the ridiculous and disgraceful sight that I will show you. Zeus's daughter Aphrodite is always dishonoring me because I am lame. She is in love with Ares, who is handsome and clean built, whereas I am a cripple – but my parents are to blame for that, not I; they ought never to have begotten me. Come and see the pair together asleep on my bed. It makes me furious to look at them. They are very fond of one another, but I do not think they will lie there longer than they can help, nor do I think that they will sleep much. There, however, they shall stay till her father has repaid me the sum I gave him for his baggage of a daughter, who is fair but not honest.

"On this the gods gathered to the house of Hephaestus. Earth-encircling Poseidon came, and Hermes, the bringer of luck, and King Apollo, but the goddesses stayed at home all of them for shame. Then the givers of all good things stood in the doorway, and the blessed gods roared with inextinguishable laughter, as they saw how cunning Hephaestus had been, whereon one would turn towards his neighbor saying:

"Ill deeds do not prosper, and the weak confound the strong. See how limping Hephaestus, lame as he is, has caught Ares, who is the fleetest god in heaven; and now Ares will be cast in heavy damages.

"Thus did they converse, but King Apollo said to Hermes, "Messenger Hermes, giver of good things, you would not care how strong the chains were, would you, if you could sleep with Aphrodite?

""King Apollo," answered Hermes, "I only wish I might get the chance, though there were three times as many chains-and you might look on, all of you, gods and goddesses, but I would sleep with her if I could.

"The immortal gods burst out laughing as they heard him, but Poseidon took it all seriously, and kept on imploring Hephaestus to set Ares free again. "Let him go," he cried, "and I will undertake, as you require, that he shall pay you all the damages that are held reasonable among the immortal gods."

""Do not," replied Hephaestus, "ask me to do this; a bad man's bond is bad security. What remedy could I enforce against you if Ares should go away and leave his debts behind him along with his chains?"

""Hephaestus," said Poseidon, "if Ares goes away without paying his damages, I will pay you myself." So Hephaestus answered, "In this case I cannot and must not refuse you."

"Thereon he loosed the bonds that bound them, and as soon as they were free they scampered off, Ares to Thrace and laughter-loving Aphrodite to Cyprus and to Paphos, where is her grove and, her altar fragrant with burnt offerings. Here the Graces bathed her, and anointed her with oil of ambrosia such as the immortal gods make use of, and they clothed her in raiment of the most enchanting beauty.

"Thus sang the bard, and both Odysseus and the seafaring Phaeacians were charmed as they heard him."[5]

In his long travels after the Trojan War, Odysseus had the good fortune to land on the island where King Alcinous ruled, the island of the Phaeacians. He was treated like the great man he was and was sung

---

[5] The Odyssey by Homer, Samuel Butler translation

this story by the bard Demodocus about the affair between Ares (Mars) and Aphrodite (the moon). Aphrodite, the wife of the crippled Hephaistos (Venus?), while he was away, managed to be seduced by (or herself seduced) Ares. Helios, the sun, watched the affair and informed Hephaistos who immediately set a trap to catch the two lovers in bed together by laying a net that would hold them in each other's arms until he arrived. Again, Hephaistos, like Menelaus, is the aggrieved husband who deeply loves the capricious wife and is deeply hurt by the affair. He decides not to give her up, but to force Ares to "pay" for what he has done, turning her from an adulteress into a prostitute. Eventually, after proper payment, Hephaistos regains his wayward wife.

All of the same elements we find in the Love Song are found in the story of Menelaus, Helen and Paris. The only difference is that in the Iliad, the actors are supposedly real living people who are inadvertently reenacting the roles established by the gods. The story of Helen is embellished with the background of a major war, a "net" of a thousand ships, lots of other colorful characters and mythical themes, even the direct involvement of the gods.

What does this story mean for us today? The Hephaistos paradigm represents for man the cuckold, the rejected, the alienated and the victim of mankind's dreams, visions and subconscious mind. Menelaus is, for us, the individual as religion has defined him. He is the long suffering lame one that has been harmed, not by society, but by the selfishness and lust for pleasure of Helen and her lover. Menelaus is modern man. Yet, his anger and humiliation force him to compensate for his infirmities by concocting a clever web, a trap, to catch the unsuspecting lovers so they may be exposed for all, especially Menelaus, to see. For mankind today, that "trap" is the Battle of the Sexes religion.

The Hephaistos Complex

Humiliation is the one emotion Hephaistos feels. When he experiences it, and he always does, he runs from it, denies it and pretends it is not real. His most humiliating realization comes with the constant thought that he will never be first but always second, always an also ran, never a participant but always a loser. For Hephaistos, his hatred is always aimed at the top, the winner, the dominant person because he knows he will never be like that person no matter how much effort he expends; so he becomes fixated, obsessed with overcoming, winning, triumphing over all adversity through his intelligence and treachery. He engages in a life-long struggle, expends tremendous amounts of energy and virtually spends his youth and strength in an endless pursuit of perfection. No matter what he does, how many victories he earns, he still feels that he is beneath all other men.

Needless to say, for Hephaistos, the anger and frustration plus the insecurity that comes from knowing that Aphrodite will not behave sexually; that she will be deceptive, dishonest and dismissive of him creates tremendous insecurity. It causes intense frustration and cynicism about people and creates a motive for anger, hatred, jealousy and even despair. It assumes that people are corrupt morally and that they must be punished for being self-assertive sexually. Hephaistos becomes the brooding and controlling bureaucrat, the witch doctor, the referee, the politician, the Immanuel Kant who seeks to destroy by creating a web of control over all men.

To understand how much emotion is involved with role paradigms, we can look at the story of Tristan and Isolde, the Arthurian legend. In this version of the Battle of the Sexes, Tristan and Isolde drink a magical potion that causes them to fall madly in love setting up a tragedy of two lovers doomed by their passion. The potion represents the separation between the passions and reason which was destroyed when the lovers drank it. The Hephaistos role here is King Mark who becomes Isolde's husband while she is drawn uncontrollably to Tristan. Mark is an honorable man fated to love Isolde who cannot return his love.

Mark is weak, easily fooled and oblivious to the love affair going on without his knowledge. Eventually, once the affair is discovered, he must ensure that the love affair cannot continue, that it is thwarted and that the lovers can never see each other again. They must both suffer unto death.

On a fundamental psychological level, the realization of the power of the "sexual woman" (women who identify their personal value according to their sexuality) creates so much pain (because of inadequacy) for her "owner" that in order to deal with that pain, Hephaistos (and King Mark) must deny it. What must also be denied is the sexual power and control of the sexually attractive woman. Man was moved during pre-history, through this process of denial, to create a religious sexual morality of self-sacrifice of Beauty as sexual goddess. For

Hephaistos, a craze that was a combination of sexual desire and of denial of the fact that he could not earn her created a stillborn longing for sexual fidelity from her. This sexual love for her became his obsession and the source of his passions and addictions. Yet, his final realization, his last thought, was his sexual impotency.

In a sense, you have, in the Hephaistos role, a moral dualism; two disobedient lovers (Ares and Aphrodite), both loved and presumed to be evil, contrasted by the watcher (Hephaistos) who must define himself as either proper (good) or deficient (good). This is the source of sexual dualistic morality found both in the early tales and in many modern sexual relationships.

It is important to point out, however, that the religious source of the dualism is what makes the Battle of the Sexes into a contradiction for the men and women that are caught in its trap. The rituals associated with the religion are essentially replacements for logical thinking, and as such, they do not really help the individual man who seeks meaning and truth; they are imposed upon him to his detriment. Both roles are destructive and concrete-bound because the individuals involved in the roles accept themselves as roles (actors in a play) rather than unique individuals. This is one of the reasons for the impersonal nature of sexual promiscuity.

An interesting twist on this role is that some men, early in childhood, develop an affinity for an Aphrodite type of woman and seek, by means of a subconscious role reversal, to play her role. This man chooses homosexuality or cross dressing because early in life he learned to love a woman with the Aphrodite Complex and wanted to emulate her femininity. In other cases, he chooses the role of Ares as compensation and attempts to become a gigolo who distinguishes himself by the number of "Aphrodites" (or by the number of Ares type homosexual men) he is able to bed.

Hephaistos is a symbol for something deeper and more sinister than we might think. His is a psychological role played in a ritual that involves sexual expectations. Hephaistos is the victimized man, the deceived man, the alienated man, the cuckold, the outsider who is simple of mind, true of heart and always the nice guy that loses. He is also the one with deep seated self-prejudices based upon his fervent conviction that he is not being treated fairly. Remember, he has been maimed (by fate) in order to ensure that he is tied to a "shop" to create his masterpieces for the collective. His denial of his inadequacy leads to over-compensation and to the desperate state of mind that concludes, "I'll get them for that." He is the brooder, the man who achieves value, not because of his own earned character but from those with whom he is able to associate (the beautiful woman or the celebrity), the man driven to steal or to rob sexually, who has himself been robbed of his prized possession, in this case, his own dignity because of the deceptions of the one person that is for him the most beautiful woman in the world (usually his mother).

Many people end their lives as unhappy Hephaistosstyle characters, wondering why they are no longer loved, why they are no longer sought out, and sad that they are no longer young. Such is the result of playing roles on a stage and living our lives as if we were those roles. Such is the loss that is inevitable when we create our rationalizations through inappropriate concrete-bound roles.

The person living the Hephaistos role has the characteristic of being what I have called an "otherist."[6] He is constantly thinking, as his primary thought, about what people think of his status. This fear of others has been created by religious morality and by a cultural adherence to the idea that the individual must gain his sense of being right and wrong from others and their evaluations of him. In my book, "Behind the Ritual Mask" I pointed out that this state is the result of moral triangulation where fear of others meets moral dualism to encourage and create the self-sacrificial impulse. It creates an automatic focus on others and disables the individual's ability to think about and resolve issues by means of reason.

The concrete-bound Hephaistos is in conflict with his fear of losing Aphrodite and losing his status among others as her owner – with humiliation looming as his inevitable nemesis. What Hephaistos seeks is to re-gain and/or keep his value of self that proceeds from his association with her.

Participation in the Hephaistos role is a ritual, a

---

[6] An individual that puts thoughts of other people as paramount in his life and thought.

reenactment of the Battle of the Sexes myth from the Hephaistos perspective. As we saw from the "Love Story", what Hephaistos feels is an intense desire to be rid of the fear and vulnerability that is part of that role. When he creates a compensating personality, by developing skills in a trade, he is attempting to defeat the fear and obtain a sense of control over his life and over her.

The Hephaistos role player operates in society as if he expects to be treated unfairly by both society and by the capricious and seductive Aphrodite that he has taken as his wife and property. He learns that no one can be trusted and that the one he loves most deeply will betray and engage in acts that should be meant exclusively for him. He learns that he is vulnerable and that valuing his love is his greatest weakness. He feels he has a right to ownership of her, not because he is a chauvinist (though insecurity is the cause of both cynicism and chauvinism), but because he hopes that by feigning the right of ownership it might ease his insecurities and help control her.

Hephaistos is attracted only to Aphrodite's beauty and part of that attraction is that she appears to be readily available to any other man but not her husband. He finds a certain cathartic release in the fact that it is always possible that she will have an affair; that she will participate in the ritual of seduction and infidelity and that he will always be the watcher. However, since he is the aggrieved party, it is he that is her suffering savior when she strays, the one who brings her home (or provides a home) to wash her soiled and penetrated body. His choice, according to the "logic" of this religious ritual, in order to find the most release possible, is either to accept it and willingly help her in her wanderings or kill her in righteous anger (another way of locking the door and throwing away the key). Indeed, one way of punishing her is to watch her being ravaged to the point of suffering.

There is a point in Hephaistos's role as cuckold when he assumes that anyone can have Aphrodite but himself. When he hears other men his age brag about having other women, he projects his woman as being one of the conquests (and he may be right). That fact, and the insecurity that he feels, along with the premise that he owns the female figure, moves him to insist on complete control over her in order to ensure that she not go elsewhere for her sexual satisfaction. Once in that position, he becomes even more vulnerable, particularly if she decides to do as *she* pleases. In fact, in her role as Aphrodite, she is supposed to cheat. Otherwise, why is she so attractive to and attracted to so many men? His insecurity is her passport to adultery. After all, in her mind, it is *he* that has invented this farce called marriage and fidelity in order to control *her*. Although, she doesn't always seek other partners, she will certainly seek to make him jealous by denying him what he thinks is his by right.

The Aphrodite Complex

Many anthropologists have speculated about a prehistoric matriarchal early society where women dominated. Generally, this society was focused on a benign nature of women as mothers and nurturers. This age was supposedly idyllic, peaceful and ruled by kindness and love.

Needless to say, I think that is a caricature and exaggeration. It is possible that there were societies that were not warlike, and in which both men and women were nurturing and loving. It is also possible that before the emergence of Ares (and the many heroes who were modeled after the god) that men were not warlike and acquisitive. Archaeology may help us identify such cultures.

During the time of the Trojan war, female goddesses, mostly daughters of Zeus, were beautiful, scheming, capricious and controlling. During this period, men were decidedly in charge, war-like and supreme. Women were coveted for their beauty and these warlike men boasted of the beauties that they conquered in their battles. Helen herself was the subservient wife of Menelaus who ended her life at the spinning wheel in virtual obscurity.

During this period women, were powerful but only within the confines of a world ruled by the powerful father, Zeus. The most common religious role paradigms included Athena (Venus and Hephaistos), Aphrodite (Moon), Hera (Earth), Ares (Mars) and the diminutive speedster Hermes (Mercury). These major gods were written about, sung about, worshipped and hated for their capricious allegiances. Human females were prized for their beauties and alluring charms. They sought to emulate the goddess by using cosmetics that highlighted their seductive natures, flashing eyes, seductive smiles, sexual openness. They knew they were in a world of men who ruled with an iron fist. If she was young and beautiful, she might enjoy a life of luxury for a time if she captured the attention of a powerful man and just as quickly she could be discarded once her charms wore off.

Yet, we must not minimize the power of certain women to endure. Helen, Nefertiti, the queen of Sheba and a few other women were important influences in the world and were prized for more than their beauty. Although much is made of their exquisite beauty and allure, I think these women were about more than just sex. Some of them, like the near mythical Sheba, were powerful because of the region from which they originated. She came from an area that had a virtual monopoly over one of the most prized spices in the world. Trade deals were her forte as is evidenced by her visit to King Solomon.

Indeed, this ability to forge international alliances with powerful potentates may have been an element in their allure. If someone like Solomon, for instance, could capture her, keep her for himself, he might be able to participate in trade agreements with other nations that would make him very strong. Therefore, his efforts to impress her with his charm and wit were all aspects of his foreign policy.

The possibility exists that these women were important because of the national alliances they made possible; the trade of rare natural resources and the need to continue such trade in order to enrich kingdoms ruled by patriarchs. Helen may have come from a region where amber, spices, gold and other rare minerals were used in trade. Kings routinely married off their daughters to other kings in order to seal these alliances. In many respects these beautiful daughters were princesses in their own kingdoms and queens in their new kingdoms. It was very important that they be treated well and kept in luxury. They endured because those trade deals were important. Indeed, the kidnap of Helen may have been an effort to control and/or maintain alliances with other countries. It may have been all about business.

These factors meant that these women could not be used as chattel. They had to be respected and even feared. They had power in a sense; certainly not the power to conquer and decimate but making them angry, inducing them to complain to Daddy, could destroy important trade alliances. They were pampered, worshipped, obeyed and respected. Indeed, Helen's decision to stay with Paris may have been an indication that she found something objectionable in her treatment by Menelaus and had decided to throw in with the Trojans and ally the Hittites. Matriarchs, probably not; but powerful and revered they certainly were.

I'm looking at a picture of an actress. Her beauty is

unforgettable, her hair is black and long, her eyes, soft and seductive, her smile like Mona Lisa's smile, faint and lovely. The role she plays in the movie I am thinking about is that of "the other woman" who brazenly steals the handsome husband of another woman.

This woman is a model for Aphrodite, the seductress, who loves no one and will take whatever lover she pleases in total disregard for those men who seek to capture her and make her their slave. She is alluring, captivating and above all fickle. She uses her sexual charms to attract, misuse and reject a multitude of men and, because so, she is the subject of much jealousy, ridicule and hatred, not to mention abuse and anger. Today she is the seductive femme playing a role, the cuckoldress, the beautiful black witch and the Domme, trapped in this role, unable to recognize and connect with the real person inside of her because she believes and has been taught that she *is* the role, the image, the outer personification of female sexuality as defined by religion.

The Battle of the Sexes paradigm brings to human relationships the implicit expectation that each woman must sacrifice herself for the sake of a man. When she doesn't, anger and jealousy "justifiably" burst out of the perennially insecure man. When she insists that she will do as she pleases, this turns the man, either into a jealous, murderous brute or a cuckold, the weak slave to her capricious nature. The disappointment, the frustration and the anger of the man who cannot manipulate "his" woman are the sources of religiously-based male dominance and jealousy. This religion is lost to us, most likely because Christianity and Islam both sought to suppress the sexual component of early religions and human relationships; but if we look at Greek mythology we find remnants of the religion of the Goddess in stories like the Iliad, the Odyssey and others.

The roles played by Helen and Aphrodite in mythology have laid the foundation for the seductive woman and for many a woman at some point in her life. In history, they were the Jezebels, the prostitutes, the mistresses, the spies and the "other woman"; each so powerful in their seductive charms that they were able to bring down nations and change the course of history. They were women who had been taught that in order to succeed they must attract and use men. Most men, on the other hand, are taught that this is the kind of woman that is desirable, irrespective of whether she has a mind or an ounce of wit. These are the kinds of women for which these kinds of men leave their wives. You don't bring them home to mother; rather you assign them to Hell to suffer for their treachery. These are the women who leave their husbands for younger men. They receive criticism for doing so and are presumed to be rebelling against the "property rights" of the husband.

The jealousy, frustration and cynicism felt by Hephaistos, because of his inability to keep and hold a female, create both tension and fear for him, more of the feeling that he is not right and that he will never be right. This feeling is so uncomfortable that he must deny it because expressing anger over his failure will unleash serious damage upon the desired object and/or ruin the relationship. Religious sexual morality and marital fidelity that demand the female sacrifice herself for the male become then the rationalizations and expressions for this denial of anger and jealousy. All moral arguments aimed at women become arguments demanding self-sacrifice by the woman for the sake of the individual who desires her. The female figure, who has become marginalized and "trained" not to do anything that would enable her to survive on her own, can only wonder how best to use her "charms," how best to "act" in order to ensure her survival through the ignorant "brute" who alone has the right of self-assertion.

Ironically, once a woman becomes married, she becomes domesticated, the female form of Hephaistos; she becomes Venus, the mother figure whose only purpose is to have children – either way, she has no choice but to have an affair or be left by her man for another woman.

Consider what Menelaus must have done to Helen after he recaptured her. He must certainly have punished her severely if the Odyssey is any indication. In this book, she has clearly changed her tune once she is back in Sparta. Again, this is a result of the fact that women, in the Greek culture, were relegated to roles where they were mere objects for use by men. An intelligent woman of that time knew that in order to survive she must submit to a brutish man. Consider that Menelaus could never trust Helen again and that the rest of her life must have been spent appeasing his jealousy – while he had complete freedom to do as he wished with any woman he wanted. She must have led a lonely and alienated life. This points out that the Battle of the Sexes paradigm does not allow a loving relationship and mutual respect between two people. If she accepts the role of Aphrodite, she learns that men are foolish and easily manipulated by her charms, that they submit only to sexual flirting, flashing eyes, sexual availability and sexual innuendo – to her all men are fools. To Menelaus, all women are sexually available, just as Helen was available to Paris when she rebelled and then again available to him once he had recaptured her.

The philosophical significance of the seductive goddess is found in how she relates to the three dominant philosophical premises found in our culture. From a religious perspective, the seductress is too free, so much so that men are relegated to controlling her by means of force. Faith always leads to force and the female gender has always experienced disenfranchisement and control at the hands of men who considered that they were doing what God demanded against the "sinful" woman.

From the skeptical philosopher's perspective Helen is a symbol for wanton, uncontrolled sexuality without standards, reason or morality. The skeptic has no foundation in morality and, under this premise, anything goes morally. The sexually free woman is left, again, disenfranchised and dead upon the pyre of sacrifice to the Gods. She is too beautiful for men so she is given to the gods (and their priests) as

Helen was given to the spinning wheel.

Reason, on the other hand would reject the entire edifice of religion as well as the artificial roles that it demands people accommodate. Reason holds that women can be individuals, that they are capable of reason, choice and that sex is not an indication of evil but the highest compliment a woman can pay to a man who earns (through reason) her devotion.

The Ares Complex

As Hephaistos has a need to impress others, because of his alienation, we have in Ares, the person who is involved in the illicit affair with Aphrodite, another form of moral dualism because he, after the affair, is placed "outside," never to be allowed to enter the sanctuary of love again. Once there, Ares switches position with Hephaistos who has successfully removed him from the picture by embarrassing him in front of the gods. Even though he is the "victor" he is also the one is despised, hated and envied because of his unscrupulous behavior. He is further minimized when we learn of various affairs by Aphrodite with any number of other gods, some of whom are quite nondescript.

Yet, at the same time, Ares is the warrior, the healthy champion who does what he pleases, the conqueror and the dealer in death. He takes Aphrodite, uses her, pays his fine and then moves on, leaving her to deal with the aura of being a vixen and a seductress, who controls Hephaistos, who is not man enough for her. Mars is the gigolo, the athlete, the champion who always gets the girl but never keeps her. He is unaware that the role he is playing is a dead end that lasts as long as his stamina allows.

Ares may also be the model for other gods such as Atlas, Hercules, Samson and even Prometheus. In short, he is the model for the suffering savior discussed in my previous book, Behind the Ritual Mask. As such he is not only a ravager of women but, in another aspect, the savior of mankind.

Sublimation is the refocusing of physic energy away from negative outlets to more positive outlets. Perhaps war, for Ares, is based upon the need to sublimate sexual frustrations and confusions. Ares is the physical one, the one with stamina and the ability to dominate and kill at will. He has little in the way of mind and more in the way of physical strength and prowess. Ares is the one sent to the wilderness. No wonder he comes back at the head of an army of other jocks for vindication. For him, the world is like Aphrodite, fickle, capricious and manipulated by whoever looks at her and says, "You are mine." Whether it is a woman or a city makes no difference to Ares, the world is feminine and his to use.

Sublimation of traumatic experience for Ares takes place in three ways: communication, ritual and warfare. Communication, in this case, requires rationalization and deception, a reversal of cause and consequence by means of creating a false metaphysical view that the world nothing but conflict. Ritual is a way of reenacting what is constantly beneath the surface, the frustration and confusion caused by religion, role playing, altruism and prejudice. Ritual reenacts the original mythology and creates a rationalized catharsis. Aggressive war is the rationalized effort to dominate all people, but more than this it establishes Ares original persona, his heroic status as a savior of mankind. Yet, it is also a cynical assumption that all people are fickle and must be overtaken because they cannot be convinced that Ares's rationalized justifications are valid.

It can be said that within the context of religious paradigms communication and war are rituals. This is indeed true because these rituals are engaged in a non-thinking, rationalized way and they impart a false sense of value. However, because rationalized communication and rationalized aggressive war are so devastating to and dominant in our culture, I feel it is important to single them out as particularly powerful acts based upon paradigmatic roles – the mystic and the warrior, one that conquers with lies and the other that conquers with weapons. They represent a pact between a certain type of Hephaistos and Ares, each of which conquers the feminine in different ways.

Aggressive war, a ritual, is a tool, only one tool, of denial. For Ares, the fact of being alienated, because of his anti-social nature, creates fear of others and deep discomfort, usually in the pit of his stomach. Because of the extreme nature of this fear, Ares will sometimes minimize it through sublimation (sexual interludes) and he learns to rationalize his fears by calling them "butterflies" and "sick stomach." What Ares feels and what causes his anxiety is fear of the opinions of other people that he has learned from parents and peers.

For Hephaistos, war, a ritual, is a tool, only one tool, of denial. For Hephaistos, the fact of being alienated, because of his jealousy of *Her*, creates fear of others and deep discomfort, also in the pit of his stomach. Because of the extreme nature of his fear, Hephaistos will sometimes minimize it by pretending to switch roles and become a dominator through trickery, deceit and lies. He will convince people to "be good" and to submit to him through fear of moral judgment and submit to Ares through fear of death. What Hephaistos feels and what causes his anxiety is fear that he will never be a man and that his current role is imposed upon him by others and that his greatest accomplishment is to make fools of them all and to watch them walking silently and chained as they are thrown upon the sacrificial pyre.

Though there is nothing wrong with the person trapped in the Ares role in a genetic sense; what is wrong is that he thinks there is something wrong with *him;* he thinks that he is the subject of ridicule and he thinks that others are critical and aware of his low moral stature. This is anthropophobia in a sense, but culturally induced and given strength by prejudices extant in cultural paradigms such as the Battle of the Sexes, the roles that individuals are forced to play. He accepts the role of Ares the warrior as his coping mechanism. At the very least, he has the power to kill.

An Ares, so consumed by fear of the opinions of others, will do whatever he thinks will get rid of the base fears, anything to be like others, even if it means having no integrity. But since Ares is discriminated against for his power, he learns to overcome his fears by using his power. He rationalizes that he is a "suffering savior" who must save the world by conquering it. He is so afraid of the opinions and ridicule of others that he would do anything to rid himself of the anguish of fearing them – so he kills them and tells the world they deserved it.

His dalliances with the flighty Aphrodite are an extension of his nature as Ares, the dominant one who believes all people are feminine and therefore subservient to him. This includes Aphrodite's husband that he ridicules and embarrasses by taking so easily what "belongs" to him. Does he care for Aphrodite? Only for as long as he is pursuing her. After conquest, the object becomes meaningless and he merely pays the fine and moves on to other conquests.

The Principles of the Battle of the Sexes

The Battle of the Sexes myth is fraught with several principles that violate the human mind and human relations. This situation is endemic in religion because its basic goal is to postulate the existence of deities that have no referent in today's world. Since these deities are not real today, any idea derived from them is necessarily wrongly based. Each of these principles illustrates this point.

Principle #1 – Human Conflict is Inevitable

The first principle for the person caught up in religious role paradigms is the principle that conflict between people is to be expected. Such an individual becomes convinced that the universe is made up of a dualism where the forces poised against him are righteous and angry. This creates chronic fight/flight/freeze responses and places the individual on the level of the animal, reacting to fear and developing a reactive morality represented by his need to control the feared others and to compensate for his/her inadequacies.

If the fight/flight/freeze response is experienced chronically, it creates chronic pain in the body. The pain is the anxious expectation of anger, hatred or discrimination from other people. Yet part of the chronic fear is based upon the cynical recognition of the futility of hoping that people will sacrifice themselves, especially women who are sexual.

The fundamental expectation is the belief that all women should sacrifice themselves for the sake of a man. When a particular woman does not sacrifice to religious injunctions and chooses to pursue sex with a number of men, she is ridiculed as a wanton woman, an Aphrodite. This is part of the effort by Hephaistos-leaning men to manipulate her. When a male is unsuccessful in manipulating her, he feels tremendous tension and becomes trapped in the Hephaistos role.

The inability of Hephaistos to manipulate Aphrodite causes more anxiety for him because of the increasing frustration and humiliation that comes from the fear of the opinions of others – fear of the chorus that watches the drama unfold. The need to react in some way, to express sexual tension with other women – to cheat, so to speak is one way of sublimating his emotional frustration over her promiscuity; his metaphysical inadequacy. What a man communicates when he cheats on his wife is that he expects or wants her to cheat on him, perhaps even let him in on her cheating. At least, in that way, he can control her actions since there was never any doubt about her sexual freedom.

The worst aspect of the Hephaistos complex is that, when facing his role, when confronting his alienation from others, when deciding how to negotiate with the world, when trying to find a way to deal with the brutal truth that he is not "one of them," a young person with the Hephaistos complex may choose to control, manipulate or brutalize other people as an expression of deep seated frustration at being marginalized by humanity. This creates dictators, mass murderers and, in some cases, politicians who are intent on harming as many people as possible, on "getting back at them" or "showing them" that he is not the loser he thinks they think he is.

Yet most people with the Hephaistos complex live lives of quiet desperation, content to work day-by-day at a fraction of their potential, content to let the world marginalize and manipulate them. These are the safe ones, the properly ritualized ones who never disagree, never disobey and never get out of line. Some find themselves in old age, bent and decrepit, unaware of the fact that they have been a player of a role and that their entire life has been that of an actor on a stage. Others, and these are rare as well, find themselves shedding their clothes and running down the street in a final expression of the sheer futility of "holding it all inside." What they hold inside is their subconscious and denied conviction that they have no right to exist.

Principle #2 – Intellectual Limitations of the Role Paradigms

Is it possible that human intelligence is affected by the degree (or lack thereof) to which men are influenced by the Battle of the Sexes paradigm? If the only points of reference for the religious mind are roles (Aphrodite, Hephaistos, Ares), in this case, how can men think outside of those roles? Can the Battle of the Sexes trap influence the possible range of thoughts the individual is capable of developing? If the context of a particular cultural paradigm is anti-thought, as those that we have investigated are, and if the paradigm is culturally dominant, then the range of intellect it would allow would be limited. Further, since ritual is essentially a reenactment, is not every act taken within the context of the Battle of the Sexes paradigm, an aspect or outgrowth of that repetition? Does it not then preclude the possibility of reason in that individual's life, at least in the areas of his/her sexual choices and sexual identity? Indeed, it must then relegate the effort by Hephaistos to "out smart" Ares and Aphrodite to a limited range of treachery. That they are not smart enough to anticipate his limited responses is another indication that the roles are intellectually limiting of man.

It is possible that religious role paradigms are the cause of emotion-driven lives that lead eventually to addiction. For instance, Battle of the Sexes role paradigms are fraught with intense emotions often suppressed or expressed through sublimation. The result is a personality moved psychologically through what it assumes is normal. Emotion drives action which does not always involve reason. If emotion is taken for granted as normal, the individual thinks negative action is normal. The individual does not learn how to check his emotions and therefore his needs. Since these needs are based in sex/pleasure, the individual develops an addiction to them that cannot be checked by reason. Since the only "logic" he has is based on an "uncheckable" emotion, the individual's choices become automatic.

Principle #3 – Sexual Dualism

The Battle of the Sexes cultural paradigm is extremely powerful because it provides a framework that, when combined with the chorus (the fear of others), the Suffering Savior paradigm and the good/evil paradigm (see Behind the Ritual Mask), leaves the individual no option but to live his or her life trapped within religiously-oriented roles.

In my book, Behind the Ritual Mask, I mentioned that the study of how the good/evil paradigm became embedded in human knowledge is an interesting study. One could imagine that as men looked around the heavens they may have noticed the Morning Star (Venus) and saw it as the Bringer of Light and associated that with the fact that it preceded the day and brought the light whereas the Evening Star (Venus) brought dark times and evil. From there, one can imagine a series of associations that led to the full-fledged conceptual division of good and evil, light and darkness and more.

Ritual is an authorized release from a state of moral paralysis. It is a form of unconscious living, repetitive reenactment rather than reasoned action taken by choice. It invalidates the individual while at the same time it releases him to act a repetitive role that is presumed by religion to be good action. The result is a "pretended" person morality, an "acting out" whose foundation is ritual – because man has not been allowed to develop his thinking abilities, his conceptual faculty. His ritualized personality is therefore false; the result of an effort to pretend to have a personality by acting a role in a prescribed way.

When a person is trapped in the Hephaistos complex, for instance, the denial of it becomes Hephaistos pretending to be Mars or Aphrodite. This creates internal sexual dualism, a psychological false alternative within the individual; the principle of anti-thesis where one side of the body is engaged in denial of one role and the other side is a pretense of another; with each side fighting the other within a strong sexual context.

Cultural paradigms encourage dualistic battles within the individual that is influenced by them. Whereas the suffering savior paradigm pits the individual against a false role, the role of the suffering savior, the Battle of the Sexes paradigm, because it is a battle of sexual roles, creates role dualism. This is inner conflict that I call moral dissonance.

Sexual role dualism takes a physical toll on the individual because if leaves him or her hanging on the edge of what someone else does, says and thinks. In effect, the individual must develop a pre-planned action response to every contingency and must exert himself as events unfold, and, since the individual fears intensely what others will do, his sexual identity is defined as a reaction to the roles and the actions of other role players in his life.

The Battle of the Sexes religion brings about several possible combinations of sex roles and personalities. Each of the roles is bisexual – in the sense that both male and female humans have the capacity to play either role. In this sense, it is very common for some men to play the role of Aphrodite by being sexual and seductive and for many women to play the role of Ares by being aggressive and dominating. By the same token, either sex can be cuckolded by their partner and take on the characteristics of Hephaistos.

Some of these combinations involve bisexuality and homosexuality such as when a Hephaistos role or Mars role chooses as one part of the dual role that of Aphrodite.

Mankind developed these sexual roles purely as an outgrowth of the Battle of the Sexes paradigm – as an outgrowth of a now forgotten religion that was at once dominant in prehistory. It is also possible that somewhere in the past, mankind (or his precursor) may have actually been hermaphroditic where the sexual roles of dominance and submission were optional and interchangeable but part of the physical makeup of the pre-human creature.

Perhaps scientific study and new discoveries may clarify this possibility; it is possible that hermaphroditic people among us may actually be clues to the nature of pre-human creatures that were made up of both sexes, people that may at one point have been selected out as sexual undesirables. In other words, the Battle of the Sexes paradigm may, in prehistory, have actually created the sexes (as they are today) through the process of natural selection and genetic adaptation of which we are not now aware.

Another implication of the fact of these switching roles is that what have been considered "divergences" from normal sexual roles can find a new explanation. Leaving aside the possibility (for some the fact) that sexual role tendencies are genetic, it is also possible that they are chosen at a very early stage in life under the influence of parents and peers. This means they may be psychological or subconscious but still "chosen". This is an avenue that should be pursued because it may help people better understand how their sexual preferences were developed, that their true sexual personalities may be entirely different from their culturally induced sexual personalities and that it was not a "moral" choice (meaning it was not immoral) at all but something that could be understood and corrected (meaning the individual might then be able to "re-think" it all and choose again.

Moral sexual dualism is a major element in the battle of the sexes religion and creates an internal battle that leads to a crisis of sexual identity. When an individual is "dualized", as I call it, it is the collective that assigns roles to him or her, the chorus, peers, the father or the mother that surround the individual. The individual may think the role assigned to him is "good" but "weak" and then he may choose a different sexual role that is "bad" but "strong." Reconciling these roles is virtually impossible and affects the individual's views on the nature of good and evil and also pits him against himself. He may try to defeat (sabotage) his own assigned roles because he does not want to be 'bad" in order to win a particular contest, or he may develop a prejudice against all people who are "good" because they are also, in his mind, weak.

On the other hand, if he views his assigned role as that of "bad" and weak, you may see the development of a fake sexual dualism that has full authority to function but, for some reason, just doesn't feel right, just doesn't work for the individual. You also find a form of sexual dualism in the role of Aphrodite who becomes alienated and punished for her "sins" and "seductions." You may also have in the role of the Hephaistos male a person who sometimes becomes a male Aphrodite through homosexuality. Another form of Hephaistos, the cuckold, may strive to be his alter-ego Mars through aggressive action as compensation.

You also have many combinations of roles where the denied fears and pretenses are reversed and then reversed again in a quagmire for the individual who is struggling to know how to fit in with the collective that rules him. There is such ambivalence and equivocation about these issues that the good/evil paradigm is often used as a thinking method where every individual, every value choice, can be justified through a sexual role combination. The upshot is that the Battle of the Sexes paradigm has replaced logic as a method of thinking since all one need do is rationalize a role at any given moment and thereby "fall" into a set of rituals that fit the roles. This is what I call rationalized role playing; truly a battle against the true person beneath the sexual roles.

Another derivative of the good/evil paradigm as it relates to the Battle of the Sexes religion is called patrism versus matrism or patriarchal society versus matriarchal society. This is essentially a division that could go either way when it comes to defining good and evil. However, history assumes that once societies are founded on this basis, that patriarchal societies tend to be based upon the idea that all sin is sexual which leads to some of the most perverse cruelties, sexual practices and persecution of women. An interesting side note is that patriarchies tend to be highly focused on suppressing sexual expression whereas matriarchies tend to be inclusive and less perverse.

Many people think that the good/evil split and the mind/body split are an outgrowth of Platonism's essences/reality split. To many minds this is true, however, I contend that the source is the Battle of the Sexes religious paradigm and that Platonism is an outgrowth of it because it starts by postulating the existence of gods and pits them against men.

Yet, we can't help but notice that this fallacious split in human thinking has done serious harm to man's mind coming from its source in prehistory to its modern manifestation in Kant's "thesis/anti-thesis split. One could say that both Kant and Christianity (that he tried to save) are responsible for carrying morality into a series of devastating false choices.

Look at the Renaissance, which was the liberation of man's mind from many of the shackles of Christianity. During this period, human freedom meant not only reason but surprisingly, according to the Church, also sexual abandon and whim worship. This was in keeping with the Church's view that sex was evil. The Renaissance represented a liberation from the Church's view of vice. It was, in a sense, a reaction to the restrictiveness of religious sexual views. The rebellion was incomplete because the Renaissance was not able to develop a moral system based upon reason. Despite this, the Renaissance liberated the role of reason in man's life including its role in his sexual relationships.

Later, Kant led to Hegel and Hegel led to Marx where success meant moral corruption and whim worship. Despite the successes, creativity and exploration liberated by the Renaissance and the capitalist era, Kant and his minions succeeded in destroying it.

Indeed, one of the key mistakes of the mind/body split, as it was reflected throughout the Renaissance and the capitalist era, is that their view of morality missed the value of reason and, as a consequence, denigrated free moral action based upon rational choice and mischaracterized it as immoral. The result is that neither Kant nor the Church were able to offer a viable moral code. They left men with the choice of either being wanton, short-term conquerors rather than long-term producers of value. The result was collectivism, gangsterism, political corruption and theft. The result was the dominance of a view of man that said he should be pious and subservient (good) rather than barbaric (evil). Never let your enemies define your moral code.

In fact, the ire felt toward the Church during the Renaissance was significant but also based upon the Battle of the Sexes religion. Taylor informs us:

"The beginning of Lent was marked by a festival resembling the Roman Saturnalia, but more violent.

Anthony Munday[7] describes it thus:

'During the time of Shrovetide, there is in Rome kepte a verie great coyle, which they use to call the *Carnevale*, which endureth the space of three or fowre dayes; all which time the pope keepeth himselfe out of Rome, so great is the noyse ande hurlie-burlie. The gentlemen will attire themselves in diverse forms of apparel, some like women, others like Turkes, and everye one almoste in a contrarie order of disguising. And either they be on horseback, or in coaches, none of them on foote: for the people that stande on the ground to see this pastime are in very great daunger of their lives, by reason of the running of coaches and great horses as never in all my life did I see the like sturre.

'And all this is done where the courtizanes be, to shew them delight and pastime: for they have coverlettes laid out at their windowes, whereon they stande leaning forth, to receive divers devises of rosewater and sweet odours in their faces, which the gentlemen will throw uppe to their windowes.

[7] Savage, H. The Harleqeian Miscellany: an entertaining selection. Palmer 1924

'During this time everye one weareth a disguised visor on his face, so that no one knows what or whence they be; and if any one beare a secrete malice to an other, he may then kill him, and no body will lay hands on him; for all this time they will obey no lawe. I sawe a brave Romaine, who roade there very pleasant in his coatch, and suddenly came one who discharged a pistoll upon him; yet no body made any accoumpt, either of the murderer, or of the slaine gentleman. Beside, there were divers slaine, both by villainy and the horses or coaches, yet they continued on their pastime, making no regard of them.'"[8]

Let's make some sense of this in terms of the Battle of the Sexes religion. This festival represents some interesting dynamics. First, it could only be a reaction engaged in by people whose moral code was once more restrictive, whose lives were controlled terribly by the Church. The abandon by which festivals like this involve wearing masks so that the mask wearer could commit virtually any crime he wanted. This clearly has a sexual component, a sort of antithetical sexual morality that was caused by the Church's restrictive policies; a good reason for the Pope and other officials to get out of town. But if you think this has nothing to do with an ancient religion consider that during the time (presumably) of the events of the Battle of the Sexes there was a world-wide war during which men killed each other without control.

---

[8] Sex in History by G. Rattray Taylor, Harper Torchbooks, Page 142 - 3

This explains the murders and crimes and plunder that took place during this festival. We are experiencing here ritualized activity fostered by an ancient religion.

What then of the coaches and horses running at top speed and running over people without concern? A good mythologist might remind you that there is one actor in the story that played a minor role and that is Hermes (Mercury). Recall that with Paris, it was Mercury who accompanied the three goddesses to the beauty pageant and Hermes was mentioned as well in our Love Story as lusting after Aphrodite who won the contest. A good mythologist might also remind you that there is a myth about Phaeton who drove the carriage of the gods across the skies out of control and eventually crashed upon the earth. So our festival here is not only a rebellion against the Christian Church but also a ritualized reenactment of the Battle of the Sexes religion. The implication here is that the event of the myth of Phaeton is thought to have resulted in the indiscriminate murder of many men by the rampaging god (See Diomedes in the Iliad). Also, there is the Devil who is mentioned in association with the plague in Mackay's book, Extraordinary Popular Delusions who rides in a magnificent invisible carriage and bribes citizens with riches if they would help him spread the plague which was killing people in Europe.[9]

---

[9] Extraordinary Popular Delusions by Charles Mackay, LL. D. Noonday Paperback Page 264

The upshot of having Christians and Kantians define morality for people is that reason is jettisoned from consideration as a source of morality. The individual is thrown into a moral vacuum and must then fall into the recommended roles assigned to him by religious premises and subconscious role paradigms. If his wife cheats on him, he becomes Hephaistos the cuckold who uses his skills to fool her and trap her into the role of the cheating Aphrodite who has affairs with the unscrupulous Ares and gets paid.

Both Christianity and Kantianism have as their antithesis the faculty of human reason. Reason is their singular enemy and therefore, as they developed throughout history, they waged war against not only reason but sexuality which involves both reason and emotions as a unity within the individual. They also waged war on freedom, individual rights and capitalism, all of which represented the liberation of man and his ability to reason. In effect, by creating a vacuum in moral thinking, they created a vacuum in human happiness and sex. They literally created the chaos that releases itself in the *Carne-vale* and other festivals.

Both Christianity and the Battle of the Sexes are religions. They are distinct only from the standpoint that the Battle of the Sexes influenced the development of patriarchy which was a strong feature of the Church once it was developed. This point is important if we are to understand the source of Christian patriarchy and the restrictions that Christianity imposed upon mankind.

As an outgrowth of split roles, it is inevitable that a conflict develops for the individual wherein both personality roles work at odds against each other subconsciously (the two devils on the shoulders). Once the method of rationalization takes hold, it is used in all situations while roles shift based upon the standard of what is convenient in a given context, what will extricate the individual from humiliation, the standard being how the individual can experience less humiliation.

Sublimation plays a major role in defining the energies (negative energies) that are released in role dualism. Because all of these roles have a more intense sexual component than what is found in nature, sex becomes a constant leitmotif of everyday life and the individual finds himself pursuing roles that are expressive of the sexuality that is within him. This exposes the pornographic nature of the Battle of the Sexes paradigm that distorts sexuality for most people. In effect, because each role requires a sexual component, sex is pursued ostensibly for its own sake so that the individual can pretend to effectively play the role he has been designated to play. Men and women become over-sexed and this has a strong influence on identity and sexual choices. Sex becomes a topic that he is always thinking about.

The complexity that sexual role paradigms create can have devastating consequences for men and women. First, the roles are artificial; they hide the true individual beneath a cover of pretension and false dealings among people. Each role is full of anti-roles, opposites that are also misunderstandings of human roles, reactions to the prejudice experienced by the individual as other people assign his position in life. The effect on human psychology is confusion, doubt and more confusion.

All of an individual's interests then become focused on resolving these sexual role conflicts and the only solution, the individual is told by culture, is to work within the context of the roles in order to resolve them – which is not a solution at all but the very trap that caused problems in the first place. Enter religion and rituals and modern psychology.

The idea of exerting oneself to "show them," to create the Hephaistos web in which he entraps his deceivers, or to prove to them that he is not an avoider, that he is not a weakling, is sexual moral dualism, pitting the individual against a presumed opposite principle. Sexual moral dualism (the sexually split individual) is a delusion. Life, properly, should be about the individual using reason against the obstacles to survival, not about the individual against a sexual role. And this is the danger of the Battle of the Sexes religion.

The psychological consequence of sexual moral dualism is that the individual sees himself as different from others because he has polarized himself against the world. Where he needs, for the sake of his sense of self-worth, to differentiate himself from others by means of his values, his dedication to reason, purpose and self-esteem. Because he focuses instead on a sexual role, he is locked into a battle for happiness without any tools that would make happiness possible. Where he needs to experience and focus on his rational love for himself and his appreciation of his own chosen values, his sexual roles lock him into fear of others. He sees himself, mistakenly, as the center of attention as did Hephaistos. The sexual moral dualist believes that he draws the focus of the world and that the world knows of his deficiency.

Once we strip away the influence of collectivism, altruism and the Battle of the Sexes, we recognize that a proper life, a life without cultural paradigms of these types, represents a much broader range of choices, all of which arise within the context of the individual's life and his necessary choices and plans. We learn that the key to a rational and happy life is to make choices based upon the individual's wellbeing (life as the standard). These are choices made without the influence of an overly sexualized role within a trap. The properly focused individual has the right and the ability to choose what he thinks, how he thinks, and what he is going to do based upon a proper standard. In contrast to the ritualized and prescribed acts of religion, these choices are made within both long-term and daily contexts. Contrast this life-serving approach against the idea that altruism is the only choice.

From a psychological standpoint, the chronic fear of other people sabotages the possibility of proper choice and morality. Fear sabotages morality because all the choices that are made from fear are predetermined by the people that engender the fear.

Most often, these actions are culturally approved ritual. Ritual based upon fear cannot possibly be morality because morality involves choice without fear, calculated actions determined by a chosen standard. This means that in our culture, within the premises of religious culture, there is no possibility of morality. For religion, morality is only altruism – a form of culturally approved suicide. For the religion of the Battle of the Sexes, morality is nothing more than sexual conquest or sexual submission. The mind has nothing to do with it.

Most people don't know they are functioning sexually under the rules of the Battle of the Sexes religion. Most are confused about their specific role and wonder why they have been forced into it and why they are treated as if they were inconsequential in their own life. Yet, tremendous amounts of psychological energy are generated as a result of self-doubts created by unchosen sexual roles. The individual becomes motivated by factors he cannot explain, whose purpose he cannot understand and whose result is unhappiness. If he refuses to act upon these "impulses" the suppressed energy needs to be released; it must be displaced and sublimated, into activities that enable the release of the energy but also allow for denial of their cause. It is the mystery religions and their rites all over again.

Principle #4 – Communication

Any culture whose members need to remember

advanced concepts must invent writing to help with communication. Writing allows the release of information that conveys where, when, what, who, how and why, all of which lead to catharsis and understanding. Writing is a tool of integration that enables man to record what he knows and remember it later when it is needed. This is why early language was pictographic in nature. Men tend to want to remember events that held deep emotional import; each pictograph represented an event and this made it important.

Ideas and concepts must accomplish something for man. They provide meaning, understanding and lead to a code of morality. Images that depict action helped men remember important events and communicate them to younger generations. Such images are concepts of action which means their purpose is to communicate moral choices or imperatives.

The individual caught in a Battle of the Sexes role must justify the denial of his trauma-generated fears. He begins to intensify his means of communication, improve his vocabulary and better express attitudes in order to communicate to others all of the ideas and thoughts that defend his avoidances and make them appear rational.

Rationalization is not rationality but a form of irrationality that uses words and mental organization to create a substitute "reality" that must be imposed upon the world in order for the denial to be workable.

If the individual can manipulate words and ideas to validate and justify his evasions and avoidances, then, he thinks, he will have "created" that reality and proven, by stealth, that he is not afraid. If he can convince others that the reality he has created through rationalization is real, then, he believes, he is closer to confidence and peace of mind. If he can find others that also accept his rationalizations, he has taken a big step toward reducing the discomfort he feels.

But there are other consequences: First, he has lost his respect for men and "learned" that they can't be trusted because they believe him. Secondly, he has also lost his respect for reality because, he thinks, it is malleable and controllable.

An example of this would be a person who is afraid of crowds. In order to "justify" his fear, he tells himself and others that people are so irrational he cannot bear to be around strangers. When others accept his rationalization about people, he has succeeded, not in changing reality but in rationalizing his fear and reversing (only in the minds of others) the relationship between cause and consequence.

The real cause of the role player's need to communicate, fear, is now rationalized out of existence and replaced by a judgment that has nothing to do with reality. He thinks he has succeeded in creating a new principle of thought; in fact, he has created a floating abstraction, an idea that has no connection to the real world. The result is cognitive blindness for himself and anyone he has convinced. From then on, he will live as if his rationalization is true and will constantly misidentify and misinterpret the actions and ideas of all men. The result is not a feeling of security but even more insecurity.

Another example of a floating abstraction, Christianity is a rationalization for self-sacrifice. We call self-sacrifice altruism today but it has existed since the mystery religions as the story of the suffering savior who struggled and died in order that imperfect man could be saved. Man's actions were sometimes seen as the cause of the anger and devastation brought upon the world by the god's and therefore the image of a god sacrificing for man became an injunction for man to sacrifice. The ritual of sacrifice was born.

Jesus was nothing more than a newer version of the earlier suffering savior role paradigm. Could Jesus have been an actual man? Not likely. There is no evidence that he was. Could he have been a cosmic entity? Possibly; or he may have been a composite of a number of real characters, probably created by Josephus, Paul and other Romans after the fall of Jerusalem in the first century.

Candidates for the real Jesus are Lazarus, Titus or even Julius Caesar in some circles. The point is that Christianity is communication of previously established myths, the development of new role paradigms that were essentially based upon old role paradigms such as the suffering savior, the good/evil split and the chorus.

The communicator or the rationalizer, in this case, is Paul the Apostle, who was responsible for spreading the Jesus myth and communicating the rationalizations that set the foundation for Christianity. The result is a belief in miracles and stories that have no basis in reality. Cognitively, man is basing his life on floating ideas.

Because the evasive communicator is "word-oriented" he tends to gravitate toward careers that involve communication, writing, sales and even management of people. As he improves his skills, he is able to minimize the power of his fears by further burying them through the success that word-usage achieves for him. That success is measured in the number of people he is able to motivate toward his rationalized and false reality. The consequences for him, however, are artificiality, narcissism, relationship confusions and eventually self-destruction. Since he cannot suppress his role within the Battle of the Sexes, which affects word usage and choice of topics, thinking and life-context (everything is about sex and sexual conflict), and since, for him, communication is a means of obtaining a false sense of self-value, a reversal of cause and consequence, there is a constant decline for this person as he descends into creating ever newer rationalizations and the expression of ever more cynicism about people – his chauvinism becomes more and more obvious.

Principle #5 – Ritual

In religious societies, ritual takes the form of repetitive action designed to reenact a myth. Ritual is the acting out of a myth rather than its emotional expression through words which is known as story-telling. However, the moral of the story that is found in almost all ritual is the same: "good, meaning the suffering savior, (based upon the good/evil paradigm) always wins." The suffering savior, because he represents a cultural institution, becomes a cultural role paradigm, an example that is transferred from myth, drama and story-telling into a moral premise for everyday human action. Society, traditional family ties, mother, father, peers, etc., create the foundations upon which cultural role paradigms are transferred to the individual.[10]

With ritual, the characters are represented by figures of monumental power and influence. Rituals reenact the lives of the gods and enable the individual to express his base fears and sublimate them so they are mitigated. Sublimation is the act of using ritual to turn base fears into a benign message with a positive morality. Ritual is designed as a collective outlet wherein the individual is allowed to release pent up tension through a collective dance. Because the collective is deemed to be the source of knowledge, the reenactment of ritual leads to "catharsis" – the individual comes out of the ritual experience satisfied and more serene and with a positive feeling (pretense) that enables him to move forward and help

---

[10] See "Behind the Ritual Mask" by the author

mankind. Ritual is social control aimed at the goals of religious authorities.

For instance, man (Hephaistos) rejected by Aphrodite, sublimates his frustration at being rejected by creating a web of ideas and words that convince others that he is not afraid, not frustrated, not a failure. He convinces them that he is really a rational man, a good man that does things for others such as convincing them to follow the precepts of religion. Guilt joins individual social frustration and creates altruism and self-sacrifice. Altruism joins the chorus and creates collective morality. Collective morality joins the good/evil paradigm and you have a world-wide religious movement.

Analysis

How does one psychoanalyze a culture or an individual who functions within the rules of religious cultural role paradigms?

One can attack the problem from a number of perspectives.

- One perspective is to understand its source in fear of others. One can learn the true nature of others, their level of cultural and subconscious premises that they take as knowledge. From that, one can identify their ineffectuality in the individual's or culture's life.
- One can also attack the problem from the source of inappropriate roles by identifying the artificiality of the role characteristics that are not inherent in the individual but are assigned by the religious roles; i.e. the examples of Hephaistos, Aphrodite and Ares, the suffering savior, ritual mask and chorus.
- We can also attack the problem from an understanding that denial is denial of the humiliation felt by the imposed role and the characteristics assigned to the role; all of which have little to do with the individual and his true characteristics. In other words, the presence of psychological denial may indicate the influences of an inappropriate role model. By helping this individual identify the inappropriate characteristics of the role paradigm, analysis can help him or her disassociate from the role and discover his true nature. Once the

individual learns that it is the non-applicable role that he is denying, he can learn to release himself from it and find relaxation. Once he learns that the role is not "him", not real and not inherent in him as an individual, he can learn to escape from it.

- Further, we can attack the problem from an understanding that each role in these religious and mythological paradigms has a duality (split personality) and that pretense is used to try to take on the characteristics of another role within the paradigm. Whether it is a pretense of anger that seeks to trap Ares (and make him pay) or punish Aphrodite (and lock her up), the alter-ego, so to speak, is merely another role and just as artificial as the original role example that the individual is attempting to deny.

- Finally, we can attack it from a more global approach and recognize that no religious role and ritual is valid, they are all prejudice and invalid and all the tension associated with them must be sought out and relaxed.

All of these points represent different approaches, each of which can be used by the individual and the analyst to improve and return to a conscious connection with his true nature. These roles create identity crises for the individual and destroy the individual's ability to function in a world of other people. Not only is the individual suffering from an individualized identity crisis, but that crisis is created by cultural role paradigms.

Once one begins to understand the different culturally

imposed roles and how they interact to create internal dualism (the split personality) one can develop a powerful solution to a large range and number of psychological problems. It is the individual that has attached importance to the opinions of others. That mistake made the individual vulnerable to the chorus's imposition of a specific religious role that had more to do with religious goals of control rather than self-understanding and happiness. They *make* one the cuckold or the seductress or the warrior. The inapplicability of the role and the rules that proceed from a moral statement of what is not possible to one within that role is what creates the individual's conflicts and doubts and inability to decide correct action.

Religion as Entertainment, Entertainment as Religion

When we look at our modern entertainment stories, particularly those that are epic reenactments of ancient myth, we find a clear dualistic ritual where evil is portrayed as ruthless, intelligent and powerful and good is portrayed as innocent, struggling and fearful. This ritual is influenced by what I call the good/evil paradigm or moral dualism. Its result is rationalism, the idea that two realities exist, one of ideals and perfect and one of this world and imperfect. Catharsis is achieved by the watcher of these stories, man, who is encouraged to face his basic religion-induced fears by watching the suffering savior struggle against tremendous, almost overwhelming, obstacles in order to prevail and save man. These stories are derived directly from the mystery rites and are reenactments of the very same stories reenacted within the context of religion.

The critical difference between ancient myths and modern stories is that in modern stories fear comes not just from a malevolent universal struggle but from other people, those deemed evil and opposed to man. This is an outgrowth of the prevailing skepticism that sees man as fallible and imperfect. Catharsis is the result of reliving the drama (as it is played out to resolution) by the watcher (Everyone is Hephaistos in this sense) and by the confronting of fear, albeit in a sublimated form, and also by learning a lesson that will make the watcher stronger, wiser and better able to understand and control his life (in our context, to be an altruist). Such is the nature and purpose of both modern fiction and the mystery rites.

As we have seen, moral dualism in these stories is based upon false alternatives that do not exist in reality. Human evil is not powerful and all-knowing but small and weak, a result of ignorance or weakness and envy. The good is portrayed as innocent, lacking knowledge and vulnerable. We have accepted these false alternatives and prejudiced ourselves against normal people by assigning religious caricatures (roles) to them.

As the above paragraph indicates, not only does moral dualism give us a false view of evil, but of good as well. This causes us to glorify and idealize an inferior level of knowledge that has yet to rise to the level of worldly experience and wisdom. The "purity" of the good in these stories is vacuous and bereft of the ability to learn anything more than to emulate living for others, as if this "altruism" was proper and correct. That loving others is only an aspect of life that must be subjected to the knowledge derived from reason, that learning proper action must be derived from reason and that proper thought means learning new knowledge, gaining new wisdom and deriving human solutions from new evaluations has been lost because moral dualism has defined the good as essentially ignorant.

Because fear of people is a metaphysical issue (people are part of what is real), fear is experienced as metaphysical or relevant to life. Since people are the reality for a young individual who is bombarded with cultural paradigms, metaphysical fear; the fear of something terrible happening, is the central focus of the individual, it is a recurring thought that will not go away, especially if it is being denied. The individual can only learn not to fear certain people but he cannot unlearn how to fear reality in general except by acknowledging the relationship between metaphysics and fear that religion has inculcated within him.

In fact, much of modern philosophy, with the exception of Aristotle's logic, is based upon the emotive expression of ritualized myth but in the form of metaphor and rationalization. Indeed, to say that much of modern skeptical philosophy is rationalized religion is an incredible truism. That much of modern entertainment is a religious activity is also true. I have pointed out before that the acts of going to a mystery rite, a play, a ball game or a movie are essentially the same as going to church. Indeed, in each case the story is the same.

The Source of Pornography

Because there is a sexual aspect to the story of the Battle of the Sexes and since sex is an element of all thinking within the paradigm, we could say that the Battle of the Sexes paradigm is the original religious source of pornography. Because of the influence of the role examples in the lives of people trapped within them, it becomes difficult for people to make proper decisions in the area of sexual choices.

It is as if the Church saw that sexuality was the enemy and strove through an emphasis on altruistic giving to eliminate the power of sex in the life of ancient man. Religious stories like Sampson and Delilah which were simply retellings of the Battle of the Sexes stories were minimized in importance in order to create a "sexless" religion.

Added to these original tales is the conversion of the "hero" from the Ares role to a sexless suffering servant. But despite these changes, people were still sexualized and strongly influenced by the original stories. Their own sexual natures, and their need to express emotions that the Church insisted they suppress, created our present pornography industry that makes lots of money in the process.

In fact, despite the wishes of the church, most individuals are still strongly affected by the pornographic element of the battle of the sexes. That affectation brings sex into the public arena as a source of collective enjoyment and even humor, much in the same way that the other gods in the original "Love Story" observed the sexual encounter and laughed. Collective enjoyment of sex and sexual humor are methods of both sublimating the base fears and intensifying both the denial and the power of sex in one's life. Publicly discussed sex becomes a method for masking deep seated fears. It is a way of getting from discussion and laughter about sex a sense of one's own value that says because I am able to discuss sex so openly, I am an adult – the equivalent of a young person smoking cigarettes in order to appear older and in charge of his life.

Within this context, sex becomes an end in itself, and for the person in denial, it takes on a life of its own, a sort of logo-motivation that gives rise to a ritual, the hunt for sex. The individual thereby learns to view sex as an aspect of life that must be understood, enhanced, developed and communicated according to certain ritualized behaviors. This aspect of the Battle of the Sexes religion is responsible for the entire cosmetic and sex industries. More deeply, it has created a form of sexual selection where certain physical characteristics are considered desirable. Women and men with sexually desirable characteristics have been those that have, for the most part, adapted and survived. The likelihood is that this form of sexual selection is responsible, over millennia, for the fact that women are generally smaller than men, more feminine and with more refined features. Generally, these characteristics have been selected by the Battle of the Sexes role paradigm that has encouraged the selection of smaller, more feminine women (Fortunately, intelligence and refinement were characteristics that also prevailed).

We must understand what I mean by the term "logo-motivation." An individual confronting the confusions and frustrations that are inevitable in a role paradigm-driven society, because cultural paradigms are subconscious examples, learns to treat these examples as if they were logos (knowledge embedded in images). These logos are memorized, concentrated upon as objects to be achieved by means of intense, driven action. Once an individual creates the desire to become an image of a sexually desirable person he becomes logo-motivated and his physical makeup and musculature becomes poised to achieve this "logo-ideal" of the sexually attractive individual. In other words, the logo-attractive individual works to achieve the image (logo) of a sexually desirable individual. Since, this motivation eventually becomes subconscious, the individual becomes ultra-sexualized because logo-motivation involves sexual "ideals." His sexual nature takes on a life of its own and he cannot stop pursuing sexual activities. This is a form of addiction or obsessive compulsion where the logos are converted to physical energy that becomes automatic and constant. In this context, the individual's sex drive becomes uncontrollable and constant. When the logos are converted to physical tension through suppression, that energy that is suppressed creates muscular tension within the individual that eventually becomes physical pain, and once that pain is numbed, it leads to physical restriction and sometimes sickness (In fact, an entire society in the grip of the Battle of the Sexes role paradigms can become sexually logo-motivated by turning over-embellished sex into a cultural institution).

In my view, the drive in both the Ares and Hephaistos males toward sexual aggressiveness involves just such a powerful logo that it creates uncontrollable sexual drives and sexual chauvinism. Because sex is sensual and physical, because sex is part of the context of everything they do, the individual must then sublimate sexual feelings and activities into 'related' activities that still help express sexual tension and energy. For Hephaistos, these related activities involve the development of productive skills. For Aries, they become athleticism and excessive exercise. Add to this a deeper foundation of what I call "Goddess worship" (that relates to earlier paradigms that have gone into the cultural subconscious) and sexuality and logo-sex becomes an ever-present factor in the life of all roles within the culture. The goddess is another logo that implies female sexuality and sexual promiscuity that are sought as a logo-concrete (the beautiful, seductive looking woman). This is why products associated with sex and sexually attractive people are so successful. It has very little to do with actual benefit in society of these products but more to do with whether they will help the buyer obtain a logo-sexual appearance and, specifically, more sex. Logo-sexuality is not sexuality; it is the appearance of sexuality that has the effect of drawing people to the user of these products.

The Sex Industry

Through his acceptance of a specific role paradigm, the fearful individual learns that he can control other people and rationalize his own avoidant behaviors through his sexual strategies. On the other hand, because he is performing a ritual reenactment of the role of the chosen example, the individual has become duped by the Battle of the Sexes role paradigm and, through this process, creates the sex industry. Notice that in the sex industry, the male is bumbling and the female is capricious. The average (bumbling) male, by means of doing business with the sex industry, has the opportunity to have a woman that is attractive and at the same time available, i.e., for sale and willing to pretend to be in love. The bumbling male (pretending to be Ares) achieves the use of the capricious female, pays his price to the pimp (Hephaistos) and moves along.

In the sex industry, there is no such thing as earning the female through projecting value; the only value is money and that buys her acquiescence and the appearance of love and passion. Like the Battle of the Sexes myth, the sex transaction is a cynical satire about the achievement of unearned value. The woman is easy, capricious and available. The man is vane, powerful and warlike. Hephaistos as the cuckold and pimp is there to take her home and clean her up. This is a completely sexualized context and the pornographic element, the idea of getting sex without having value, is what attracts men that lack self-esteem, it is what turns these men on; they are so conflicted in life that they need some outlet for their pent up energy, their denied pain and fear. Paying for sex is an outlet for pent up emotions that involve "pretending" to be an honorable man.

The Battle of the Sexes paradigm is the cause of sexual addiction; one gets addicted to something that reverses cause and consequence in morality, the doing of it gives one an illusory value or feeling. This is why so many of the pleasures an addict selects are destructive: he has divorced reason from the process of sexual choice and so anything goes as long as he gets, somehow, anyhow, the appearance or feeling of pleasure and value. What is addictive for him is not so much the power of the addictive sexual practice but the power of the need for pleasure. That engaging in sexual abandon can eventually destroy the individual is one of the side effects, one of the negative aspects of the addiction. Break the need for this form of pleasure and you break the need for "illicit" sex and other forms of addiction.

Why is sex addictive within the context of the battle of the sexes? It replaces the work needed to actually think and gain pleasure as an expression of real self-value. Addiction means a suspension of consciousness and that means a suspension of reason. The power of addiction is not so much in the power of the narcotic and the feeling it gives, it is in the power of the ease with which an individual can suspend his mind's workings, can suspend his consciousness and, in effect, thumb his nose at reality and its requirements. He may think he can do it once, but once he does it, he learns how easy it is. What is fun to do, in this context, must be done no matter what.

Likewise, man, in religiously induced denial, is full of censored thoughts and it is those censored thoughts encouraged by the Battle of the Sexes religion that encourages those roles which bring guilt. Denial is not only a method that the individual invents in order to avoid thinking negative or uncomfortable thoughts. Denial is also a method that one is taught by example, by means of seeing denial practiced by significant others when one is very young. It is all done within the context of the Battle of the Sexes religion.

Goddess Worship

For Hephaistos, sexual frustration and rejection stimulate his mental concentration and effort. This is because he has a deep-seated need to possess the Goddess, to own her and to do whatever it takes to achieve that goal – she is the source of his sense of pseudo-self-value. He is the religion-influenced driven man – driven to succeed within the context of the battle of the sexes.

To understand the source of Hephaistos's need for the Goddess, we must recognize that every human being is conceived within the walls of a woman. Her protection and nurturing is so much a part of the young being that in many ways, particularly in ways that impress upon his total dependence, she *is* him, she *is* what he is internally.

Once he is thrust into the world, he begins his exploration of life, but he is still terribly attached to her. She is an imposing presence, her every look, her every word is experienced both internally and externally. His sense of self hangs in the balance of her every word, thought and expression. In a sense, he will always need her. As he explores life, he learns that he cannot have his mother figure completely; he learns that he does not possess her but someone else does. This is not the source of jealousy if he understands that he is the offspring and not the "owner" of the mother. But his explorations allow him to apply the same needs he has of mother to other women, some of whom reject him, some of whom are unconcerned and some who are not at all like "mother." He learns to substitute for mother but he also learns that there are some tremendous challenges associated with "woman" as well as some other amazingly wonderful possibilities.

Needless to say, this is not the case with the female. Although the mother has a tremendous moral power with the young female, the female is able to emulate the mother freely and as a consequence she is able to develop a stronger sense of identity *as* a woman. There is more security in this situation. A female does not need a female as intensely as a male needs a female because the female is already a female.

The religion of Goddess worship is a hidden cultural influence that came from even earlier prehistory. From a religious perspective, she gives him the freedom to engage in several rituals (pursuit, marriage, locking her up) that enable him to pursue a female as his right. Within this religion, the Goddess is supreme, the giver of all and the taker of all, a nurturing mother and a violent, capricious, devouring warrior. He learns that his role is to worship her, to compliment her, pray to her, beg from her and submit to her. The Goddess is not only the mother of man, but the mother of the universe. To him, she is all knowing and to experience her frown causes deep anxiety so he does everything he can to please her and perform as she wishes.

For the Hephaistos role in particular, everything is about sex and everything therefore has a pornographic component. Because Hephaistos, the watcher, assumes the secondary role to a thieving

Ares, this implies the secondary sexual role. This means that every male, for the watcher, is a potential Ares and every female is a potential Aphrodite. Because the female is the dominant ideal, and this ideal has a strong sexual aspect, sexuality is part of every thought and situation. When he is not pursuing sex, he is fantasizing about it. If he is not near her, he fantasizes that she is with someone else. Once he is under the influence of the goddess, his only thoughts are of sex and her.

Sometimes, the Hephaistos and Ares males switch roles. An excellent example is the young boy who is forced by others into the role of Hephaistos. This boy, often thought of as a "sissy," is early on very trusting and open to others, so much so that he is considered a fool and often abused and insulted. At some point the embarrassment and humiliation of the Hephaistos role becomes so intense he refuses to participate in it. He becomes the alpha male, insisting that he switch places with all the Ares males he knows. This occurs through logo-fixation. This new alpha role is also artificial because he is now functioning within the rules of the Ares role rather than his actual personage. Yet, he may still agonize for his entire life that he is "really" a sissy or homosexual when in fact, were it not for the roles associated with the Battle of the Sexes religion, he would not have been placed in that position.

The Battle of the Sexes represents a "sex-based" form of early religion replete with its own orgiastic rituals and mystery rights. There is an excitement about it; sexual excitement is the natural state of the person caught within the roles. Both the context and the content of all living moments are sexual and because so the battle of the sexes roles are replete with sexual innuendo.

When the gods took on the characteristics of human beings (anthropomorphism), and this was a critical psychological mistake for mankind, the human beings necessarily gained the opportunity to take on the roles and characteristics of the gods (deification) which set up an interesting human dynamic by giving rise to Emperors who claimed to be real gods, semi-divine people and pseudo-divine men such as warriors, cuckolds and vixens. Humans could even claim for themselves a range of characteristics that were impossible such as omnipotence, omniscience, envy and capriciousness; what would have been natural extensions of normal human aspects became exaggerated and caricatured. Likewise, when certain gods function in sexual roles, sexual relationships among them, as in Hephaistos, Ares and Aphrodite (and don't forget father Zeus), then people (some people) will function in those roles through religious rituals.

This further complicated the individual's understanding of his or her own sexuality and sexual motivations and partner choices. When the culture rewards women for being alluring in places where sex should not be an issue, such as in the work place, incredible amounts of unchecked sexual energy are developed that have no release except through inappropriate sexual bantering and prejudice. When some people base their sexual choices purely upon sexual attractiveness (infatuation), there is no way to know how things will turn out.

How can the individual make decisions about values and life in such a sexually-charged state of mind? He or she must learn to suppress the sensuality of his artificial daily life and because he feels compelled to block that sensuality, unexpressed tension is pent-up and needing release. This is one reason why so many religious people find themselves caught in sexual value contradictions and why their lives are such a mess in terms of their relationships. Their mainstream religion (for instance the suffering savior) clashes with their "subconscious" religion (the Battle of the Sexes) and this conflict becomes charged with hidden sexual content, taboos and restrictions that work to build up both denial, tension and excitement. This is another way that religion creates the problems for which it offers itself up as the solution.

Logo-fixation starts as a recognition of a void; a void created by cultural paradigms inflicted on the individual by others and expressed by the individual through sublimation, converted into culturally approved action designed to overcome the perceived void. Logo-fixation is a reaction to an anti-concept, the anti-concept being the presumed inefficacy of the individual (and of every man) and once that inefficacy is accepted, the individual, through logo-fixation engages in a process of attempting to "find meaning" by fulfilling the culturally approved ritualized catharsis.

To escape from this position, as we've discussed

before, the individual must learn that his accepted role (and personality) is not the real him; is instead an imposed role that has no (real) meaning. At the very least it is a combination of his personality with the influences of false role paradigms. His proper reaction should be to find his real self and express it without regard to the machinations of cultural role control.

No amount of denial will protect an individual from the deaths of loved ones including global catastrophes of the 9/11 variety. No amount of tension will block an individual's vulnerability to the vicissitudes of life. There is no need to create a separate personality that is equipped physically to block pain; one must merely learn how to deal with and accept the "accidents" of life. The individual would be better served by facing the reality that he is vulnerable to disaster, but more importantly, learning that disaster is not the norm of life and need not be the expected.

The Trojan Horse

The Trojan Horse is one of the most unique metaphors in all of mythology. It is connected to the ritual mask of many religions because both the wooden horse and the wooden mask hide menacing men poised for destruction.

As mentioned in my other book[11], the ritual mask is merely a man who sublimates his own rationalized fear through the fear he engenders in others, just as that fear was engendered in him. The ritual mask is metaphysical malevolence expressed to an innocent person. Disapproval destroys his ability to live and creates his need to deny that he is afraid; which destroys his ability to enjoy life.

Likewise, within the Trojan Horse is hidden the hateful man, Menelaus, who was rejected by a beautiful wife in love with a beautiful man. He was the envious hater who sought to destroy that beautiful man and place that woman in a prison of self-sacrifice. Each of the characters in the Battle of the Sexes religion represents the roles that are imposed upon many of us at one time or another in our lives.

Is it possible that the people most influenced by the Battle of the Sexes religion are the least successful in life and relationships? Do they have more conflict with others; are they more prejudiced and limited in their capabilities? I submit that religious cultural paradigms and their influence on peoples' lives are one of the primary reasons for human failure. The

---

[11] Behind the Ritual Mask

idea that society makes an individual into an outsider, as occurs in all role paradigms results most particularly in the suffering savior and Hephaistos roles..

Success, within the context of the battle of the sexes role traps, is based upon conflict and winning by any means. Is it possible that those people who are the most successful in life and relationships are the least influenced by these religious cultural paradigms in the sense that they do not practice it consistently and avoid performing rituals? These happier people, feeling more entitled and free to think and do as they wish, are generally less imprisoned by cultural roles and more capable of seeing and understanding reality. Success outside of the religious cultural context is based upon reason and properly defined values as well as cooperation without conflict.

Human conflict is only a phase in human action. It is not a continuous circumstance. It is the phase before equilibrium and harmony. We misinterpret reality and the universe when we interpret conflict as the principle of all action in the moral sense. This applies to the good/evil paradigm as well as to Kant's analytic/synthetic dichotomy. Reason, on the other hand, is the producer of harmony. It is an effort to understand existence in order to harmonize man and his actions with reality and the facts. Reason creates society and freedom because all men are judging the same reality with their free minds. Conflict creates dictatorship and war because most men caught in the traps of religious roles see only conflict, hatred and their pseudo-harmony can only be reached by the death of some men.

Epistemologically, the opposite of religion is reason. Reason holds that conflict is only one aspect of reality, the resolution of which leads to harmony, and that harmony (meaning the harmony of ideas with reality) should be the fundamental goal of human consciousness. Harmony through truth, understanding and knowledge can lead to happiness.

On the other hand, the approach of religion, as an attack upon the individual is the approach that created the Dark Ages where essentially, man lacked harmony, his ideas did not conform to reality and therefore he was unhappy and conflicted. Whenever a man has in his psyche the idea that he should prohibit himself from even developing a self and that he should favor acquiescing and conforming to the religious collective, he has a form of the Dark Ages mentality within him.

The Sacred and the Profane

What is the true role of pleasure in life? What is the proper role of sex? Is sex sacred or profane? To answer this question, we must get a clear grasp of what it means to call something, an idea or and act, "sacred".

Mircea Eliade tells us:

"For the historian of religions, *every* manifestation of the sacred is important: every rite, every myth, every belief or divine figure reflects the experience of the sacred and hence implies the notions of *being*, of *meaning*, and of *truth*. As I observed on another occasion, 'it is difficult to imagine how the human mind could function without the conviction that there is something irreducibly *real* in the world; and it is impossible to imagine how consciousness could appear without conferring a *meaning* on man's impulses and experiences.'"[12]

The implication here assumes much. Although beautifully stated, we have to ask how all-encompassing this view of the "sacred" is, for indeed, not all gods are wonderful; many of them have terrible aspects, are capricious and jealous and spiteful and manipulating. They even lie and deceive, engage in illicit affairs that are fraught with infidelity. We must ask if this idea of the sacred assumes too much. Indeed, our study has shown this.

---

[12] History of Religious Ideas by Mircea Eliade, Preface, Kindle ebook version

Does the sacred involve sexual denial, jealousy and treachery? One would think not. Does it involve the destruction of large numbers of individuals such as that done by Ares and Diomedes and several others during the Trojan War? I think not.

Perhaps then our definition of what is sacred needs to be brought down to earth a bit. The sacred is experienced by man and it must therefore relate to that which is of ultimate value and depth of meaning *for* man. Man thinks of something as sacred because it is perfect in some important way. When man worships a god, for instance, he wants to worship him for his supreme goodness which means he must focus selectively upon qualities he finds meaningful in that god. Yet, this sense of meaning can often be empty because man essentially derives his concepts by means of his own perceptions and experiences. There is no way to assign content to an ethereal entity that has never been seen. We must, therefore, attain that meaning by means of faith and acceptance without any referent in reality. This makes it a deductive process rather than inductive. In fact, one cannot *induce* god.

What man can induce are things, ideas and principles by means of his experience, his rational thought and his scientific experimentation. So, with that said, the "sacred" can only involve an evaluation of things, people, ideas and principles that man is able to ascertain through direct experience and reason.

And this is the problem with worshipping gods. Man

can experience and worship a woman, for instance, because of her beauty and character as those are reflected in her being. To man, then, a woman can be sacred, she can be a goddess. He can touch, experience, see and make love to her. His feeling for her could mean that her essence is sacred for him, that she is worshipped for the value she possesses. On the other hand, man cannot experience a "goddess" in the same way he can experience a woman.

When we are born, we don't have the image of a "goddess" imprinted into our memory. The idea of a Venus, a goddess worshipped by the ancients, would never have entered our mind were it not for the fact that someone pointed to an object in the sky and told us that bright spot up there was the goddess Venus. As youngsters we might even be confused about how a thing that sparkles in the sky could represent love and nurturing and fidelity and beauty. When we study mythology and ancient religions, we might begin to understand but it is still strange to us that this thing up there could have done all the things that Venus is said to have done. How can it possibly be sacred when it just sits up there shining?

Needless to say, many arguments have been made regarding these questions including the argument that God is singular. The other Gods were anthropomorphic expressions of man's ideas and imagination. They didn't really exist. The shining objects in the sky merely have the same names as the gods worshipped by man; and since then we have advanced to monotheism. The real God is ethereal, distant but nonetheless real. So we arrive at our original question; how could He "mean" anything to me if He is so distant? How can He do miracles when that violates the laws of cause and effect? We are told it is merely a matter of faith.

As you have probably guessed, I think that a singular God is not the answer. The objections that many people have about the "gods", those vane and frivolous beings who move around in the heavens, apply equally to "God". If you can't bring God into the room, it comes back to faith and, with faith, there is no cognitive, inductive possibility.

So it comes back to the idea which has often been expressed as "as below, so above". These gods are all figments of our imagination, of our desire for universal truths as they were experienced by primitive man. Today's religions are mere expressions of these ancient ideas that have come down to us as role paradigms, examples whose only purpose is to help us understand how we should think and how we should act. They are a primitive form of philosophy. We imparted our own experiences and ideas into them and then they "reflected" back to us how we thought they thought we should act.

What, then, does this make of the "sacred"? That view of the sacred tied to gods is nothing more than a faith-based projection of what we want to believe is the source of wisdom for man and, because it is primitive, it is not enough for us today. We need more. We need knowledge and understanding that we can rely upon not just accept "God" because He is called "sacred". Yesterday's "sacred" is today's mistaken notion.

So, today's "sacred" must be something that is real, something that relates to "me", to my values, to my aspirations, to my concept of truth, of beauty and of universal essence. That's why we worship beautiful women and beautiful men; why we worship intelligence and find inspiration in feats of athletic prowess and tall buildings and even shining stars that our telescopes now help us see much more clearly than the ancients saw them. The sacred is the best in man and it includes the hardest to accomplish, the highest we can climb, the farthest we can fly, the fastest we can go. These accomplishments mean something to man.

When a man sees a rare woman, someone who "has something" few other women have, he wonders at how she became that rare, what did she think, do, say, learn and come to know that made her the way she is. That is worshipful. That is sacred. The next question for this man is whether he is up to the task of winning her and experiencing the rarest beauty of all, the moments of his enjoyment of her magnificence and her enjoyment of his. No god can give it to him. He must worship THIS goddess, the real woman who surpasses his highest values.

In my view, people are not getting enough of this kind of worshipful pleasure in life and this fact means that they have not learned to enjoy their very selves, their individualism. Is the self sacred? Yes, but we must define the self according to a standard that sees the full capability of the self, not only for seriousness but also for pleasure and happiness. Religion limits the self to the issue of service to others. It sees man as a virtual slave that must take his duty to others seriously and who must aspire to no happiness except that which proceeds from service to others. Since it is impossible for one man to successfully serve all of mankind, despair is his only logical state. The attainment of happiness, being such a personal state, is not important according to the religious definition of the sacred. And this destroys the highest possible (pleasure, joy, self-confidence, self-expression and love of the highest).

According to religion, being concerned with alleviating the suffering of the poor is more important than happiness; indeed, according to this view, altruism (charity) is supposed to be the source of a more profound happiness. Consider, however, that this view destroys the possibility of any form of happiness that is not based upon altruism and relegates sex and sexuality to the realm of profanity. This means that, according to the premises of religion, sex has no moral position – it means nothing in morality and in terms of man's value. And since sex has nothing to do with altruistic action then it is wrong. It is an animal act to be mindlessly engaged in for the sake of procreation. How mechanical and empty that is.

My view, the view that the sacred is the highest possible to man, elevates the role of reason in life and turns decisions about pleasure into personal accomplishments that generate pride and self-love. If you think that reason has no place in sexual enjoyment and sexual choice, then you do not recognize the ability of the human being, of yourself, to have a rational, value-based and enjoyable, guilt-free life. The religious definition of sex as evil makes both reason and happiness impossible and switches the pursuit of happiness toward self-sacrifice. There is no accomplishment and pride in that view. Anyone can do it.

The definition of the word "serious," once it becomes tied to the fundamental concept of "important" fixes both the religious state and the "serious" state into the mind of man as desirable, diverting him from reason and joy. Through the assignment of seriousness only to religious concepts, man is forced into an acceptance of primitive religious paradigms as singularly important.

The author is going to do something outlandish and profane. I am going to defend the individual's right to pleasure, freedom and reason, the right to develop one's mental state and knowledge by means of thinking and acknowledging the facts of reality, facts that state unequivocally that there are no ghosts flying through the universe, that there is no evidence for the existence of a "god" and that altruism, the state of voluntary self-sacrifice, is not the proper philosophy for man but the very essence of evil that has made impossible the ability of man to survive on this earth.

Reason demands that man look out at the universe

and attempt to understand what he sees with his own eyes, that he learn how to develop knowledge and use that knowledge for the purpose of survival, that production, the creation of value, is a concept that results in living, valuing and enjoying life. Reason is not about mystery, ineffable secrets, religious rites and demands for sacrifice. Reason is the faculty that enables a man to decide to do right, to do the truly "social" thing and the truly civilized act.

For a person of reason, the concept of the sacred does not involve religious elements. Value is identified according to a standard that holds man's life as the sacred. For this kind of person, altruism is only an idea that reeks of irrationality while reason is full of alternatives for solving human problems and can help man define solutions that do not require a sacrificial altar and a destruction of the best among us. Where altruism says obtain your sacred values by means of affecting others through religion, reason is the value that creates all value; reason sets the proper foundation for man and does not require that he confiscate anything from others.

The combination of the Good/Evil paradigm, the Suffering Savior paradigm, the Chorus paradigm and the Battle of the Sexes paradigm has tremendous psychological power and is, in my view, responsible for the psychological tensions that lead to paranoia, schizophrenia, the split personality and myopia. These paradigms have the power of the culture and conflict with reason.

Battle of the Sexes
1. The Love Song – Female Infidelity
2. The Hephaistos Complex – Cuckold – Revenge - Skills
3. Sexual Roles – Gender Discrimination
4. Religious Marriage as Sacrifice of Woman
5. Family Values – Marriage as Duty – Anti-Abortion – Anti-Stem Cell Research

Moral Dissonance

We have already discussed the fallacy inherent in offering altruism and collectivism as automatic solutions for every human problem. In fact, if we analyze history with the proper perspective on human value, we learn that altruism has been a problem throughout human history, not the solution.

Every major failure and war can be directly tied to altruism as the source. The Nazis, for instance, believed in the supremacy of their race, their collective, and the utter duty of all Germans to sacrifice for the sake of the race. The Soviet communists believed in the superiority of their socialist system, the workers (collective) and the requirement that the individual sacrifice himself for the sake of the collective. Almost every major religious group in history has considered itself the true religion (collective) and has insisted on the utter responsibility of the believer to perform the role of suffering savior and sacrifice for others. Political group warfare, as it is practiced in the U.S. proclaims the importance of the group and the utter responsibility of every individual member of the group to ensure its survival against other groups. Whenever you see collectivism and altruism, you find only conflict, prejudice, sacrifice and decline.

The reason that collectivism has been the dominant philosophy during periods of decline is because it brings men down. This is true even and especially with Christianity and those political systems that were derived from it, including monarchy, theocracy, communism, fascism and socialism.

Any system based upon collectivism must have complete acquiescence in order to justify using each individual to achieve its goals. Any individual who dissents is necessarily a threat who could cause others to dissent. And since the collective deems that its goals are "good", any form of dissent must therefore be evil.

What does an onslaught of collectivism and moral dualism do psychologically to the victim? One might find it strange to hear that "teaching" a person to be "good" is an onslaught, but I believe that is the case. When collectivism is the only moral option, it could be nothing but an onslaught.

One key point that has been barely noticed by psychologists is that most of the people they analyze have been victims of the teachings of moral dualism. Many of their confusions were created by cultural paradigms derived from religion. This is a testament to the fact that most psychologists are not aware of their negative nature. They can't see the forest for the trees.

Moral dualism creates intellectual ineptitude because it is based upon a misunderstanding of the nature of the universe. The moral dualist believes in a universal clash between intrinsic forms of good and evil that do not exist in the universe. This "mistake" necessarily creates a misinterpretation of the moral worth of objects and events in the world. If this does not create inefficacy, doubt and loss of self-confidence, nothing else can.

Moral dissonance is what occurs when an individual's moral "ideals" conflict with his subconscious desires. The existence of moral dissonance is seldom considered to be the result of the fact that altruistic morality is impossible to practice consistently. This means that people feel they can't be moral and that their bodies want to do something other than what they "should" be doing. The individual suffering through moral dissonance has not learned to question the difference between "faith-based" collectivist/altruist thinking and what is in his self-interest.

How can people deal with the discomfort created by moral dissonance? One option is to consider the issue too confusing and then to deny the conflict.

The second option is to recognize that both idealism and the contradictory behavior are two sides of the same religious coin. Before one can do this, however, one would have to recognize that moral dissonance is caused by cultural influences already in society.

Moral dissonance paralyzes the individual and makes him unable to decide about proper action because 1) he cannot live according to the views of his idealistic religious premises (life is impossible on such terms) and 2) the real world is where his misbehavior is taking place.

People agonize over why they keep making the same mistakes in their lives and why they seem to have no choice about doing things that are considered to be evil. The reason for this can be found in the conflict between philosophical idealism and objectivism. Idealism means getting knowledge from another dimension while objectivism means getting it from reality, the here and now.

Idealism holds up "perfect" concepts that represent the good for which man should strive. This "good" however, is not tied to the individual and his self-interest. As a result, what is really in his self-interest becomes harder to understand leading to anxiety and doubt about proper action. The only choice allowed for man is to default to self-sacrifice while his need for pleasure and enjoyment tugs at him constantly for fulfillment.

Add to this the fact that pleasure is not evil and you can understand the confusion. To be told that one should scourge oneself and force oneself to have pain as an expression of love for the deity, must certainly make the individual wonder if personal pleasure is allowed at all. Yet, the denial of pleasure actually intensifies the "need" for it. Is it any wonder that the individual develops an intense physical need for pleasure after receiving all this punishment?

Any time you are *forced* to do something you'd prefer not to do, even if you are convinced that it is good for you, your mind and body rebel against it. It doesn't matter whether that force is "morality-based" or gun-based, the very fact that you are doing something against your will is disconcerting. Even worse is to have to suppress pleasure and do something for others. This is moral dissonance and the danger is that in order to feel psychologically free, man must release all controls which could lead to inappropriate behavior.

Human Psychology and Religion

When one looks at the Battle of the Sexes myth, one cannot help but notice that it also represents a ritual about male/female relationships. And a critical question to ask regarding the influence of ritual is whether man, in the enactment of ritual, is conscious. It is certainly true that he can be aware of what he is doing when he is playing a role within a ritual "acting out". But in most cases, the individual deliberately puts himself into a trance-like state during the ritual. For most people, the decision to perform ritual is a sub-conscious or learned response engaged without critical analysis. Ritual is culturally induced.

Various archaeological sites have suggested that the myth of the battle of the sexes may have been with man since the dawn of the Neolithic (10,200 B.C.E.), which is considered the period when man as we know him emerged. In various Neolithic sites small figurines purportedly representing an obese female subject have been found. These as well as the discovery of other bull figurines indicate the presence of both Ares and Venus during religious rituals at these sites.

These findings also indicate that it is likely that man had already developed primitive agricultural societies and primitive civilizations at about the time he began to worship these gods. The likelihood is that he was already a "rational" creature at this time and the discovery or creation of gods and religion was engaged after he had developed hunting, agriculture and stone-working.

The significance of this fact is that it clarifies the point that mysticism, being based upon primitive philosophy, is something entirely different from the primitive thought processes that created primitive societies. Many ideologues for religion attempt to connect god and society as if society could not have come about without the ideas inherent in mysticism. I hold that it was likely that man was already living in primitive forms of voluntary associations before he was even confronted by the moral requirements of religious premises. Man was already a "fact-based" creature, albeit primitive, before he became aware of ideas such as faith, gods and ritualized morality.

In other words, religion was an abnormality that primitive man did not need. Man could have done fine without religion; he could have developed societies based upon a primitive form of induction, cooperative transactions and even a rudimentary justice process without a belief in deities. In fact, as we study religion and the moral processes embedded in religion, it is likely that man would have been in a better position culturally without the influence of religion. Certainly, he would not have had to deal with the psychological consequences of a belief in evil demons, destructive entities under every rock, etc. and developed a more realistic outlook on life and human relationships.

Needless to say, this view is contrary to the religionists who tell us that man could not have developed morally without religion. I think that he could very well have developed morally and that he developed pretty well before he was confronted with religion. Human psychology, then was forced to stumble into confusion under the influence of magic and spirits.

The result of religious influences then is that man is made to struggle psychologically because he was taught that a dedication to others represents the supreme moral focus; once this happens, reason is removed from the conversation and becomes an after-thought. When men think that it is evil to enjoy life and be self-concerned, they are forced into psychological doubt and wonder why they really don't feel good when they help someone who lives without an ounce of honor and self-love.

Rationalization then becomes a way of compromising with the demands of idealistic morality. Where idealistic morality demands a restrictive purity, a denial of man's worldly nature and total self-abnegation, the individual who is afraid to challenge self-sacrifice must find a way to compromise with the demand. He develops an intellectual compromise that allows him to smuggle some selfishness into his life. He develops chronic guilt and unhappiness.

With religion, the conflict for most people is between their unachievable "idealism" and what they have been taught is whim worship or selfishness. Since they have been told that selfishness is evil, they have no justification for doing that which brings life and accomplishment. Idealism is based upon floating abstractions and leads to rationalism and this disconnects man from both reality as such and the reality of the self.

The most critical failure of rationalism is its inability to offer a moral code that connects to reality and a man's individual needs and aspirations. Because the religious moral code is intended to motivate people to "be good" through sacrifice, there is no justification for self-interest in a practical sense and this results in a morality that does not work. In fact, this morality is deadly.

This reveals the danger inherent in idealism. What if the characteristics of the moral ideal have no meaning for the individual? To use an example, Jesus performed miracles. Would not my idealism of the goodly nature of Jesus then create a false person in me if I too tried to perform miracles? What if I would otherwise, without the ideal, have developed into something finer than the ideal? How would I know when that ideal is an imperative among my family and peers? Have I not then allowed the ideal to turn me on the wrong course? Worse, how many people agonize throughout their life because they are not able to live up to the ideal? How many suffer needlessly because they believe the entire world sees their unworthiness because of their "inability" to live the ideal?

Reason is not a morality. Reason is a method, a faculty and a basic set of rules designed to ascertain truth, develop knowledge and, upon this basis, define standards of action. This must be clearly understood: if one does not use reason, one has no way of knowing if one's chosen actions are correct. This means that, in reality, the moral dualist is doing something improper and even evil when he bases his actions on blind faith or a leap of faith.

In my view, most psychological sicknesses are created by onslaughts (attacks) against the individual, using altruism and collectivism as authority. The victim of these attacks is necessarily put into discomfort and begins to question his worthiness. Moral triangulation consists of using the "power" of the collective and the assertion that the individual is evil in order to move the individual, through guilt, to sacrifice a higher value for a lower one.[13]

The reaction of any animal that is attacked is fight, flight or freeze, all three of which represent the hallmarks of most psychological sicknesses (split personality, phobia and paranoia). Though the goal of such attacks is to engender altruistic self-sacrifice, sometimes the sacrificed self-destructs because of the overwhelming fear he experiences.

All forms and derivatives of anti-reason, mysticism, Kantianism, skepticism are forms of attacking man's mind. Their goal is to destroy the efficacy of man's mind and reason. Since reason is the only way to understand reality, then any attack on reason and the mind is an "attack" on man. For man, there are only two fundamental responses to these attacks: to either accept or reject the validity of the attacks. Mental health and sanity proceed from the rejection of these attacks and lead to the acceptance of reason.

---

[13] See my discussion of moral triangulation in my book Behind the Ritual Mask

Nuerosis and insanity proceed from the degree of acceptance that a man engages toward the fundamental principles of anti-reason; collectivism, altruism and man's inherent evil.

Shedding Altruism/Collectivism

Is it possible for the individual influenced by altruism and collectivism to arrive at a point in life where he does not worry what other people think? Can he ever arrive at the point where the key question is not what people think but what "I" think? Can he live in the world on his own without fear of the opinions of others?

To reach this point requires both a recognition that there is nothing to fear and that the ideal situation is to have an active mind that thinks, evaluates and makes conclusions on its own. Below are some suggestions on how one can rid oneself of collectivism and altruism:

1. Look for the results of collectivism and try to connect them intellectually to your non-verbal subconscious thoughts. This will enable you to be more conscious of the internal, subconscious process of living collectivism and give you some ammunition to combat it. Whenever you are thinking "collectively" you are thinking of others. Ask yourself if this helps you get at truth.
2. Recognize when you are seeking the approval of others and question why you are doing it. Try to connect your mind intellectually to the original non-verbal and subconscious thoughts about needing to please others and try to correct the view by asking what you need rather than what others need.

3. Look for times when you use altruism and collectivism as badges of honor and notice that you are trying to gain admiration from those badges. Resist the effort to do so and attempt to focus on the real reasons for acting appropriately.
4. When you are acting altruistically, question it. Why? To actually help someone or to gain admiration and acceptance? Why are you doing this? Engage your mind. What is the appropriate, logical thing to do, rather than the easy thing of altruism? What advances your values? Are you giving up a higher value for a lower value?
5. Notice times when you are trying to read the faces of others and ask yourself whose opinion do you want to follow, an inaccurate reading of someone else's feelings or your own thoughts. What are your own thoughts? Why isn't reality more important to you than the opinions of another individual?
6. When are you rationalizing altruism? Look for times when you are trying to convince yourself that giving up your values for others is the right thing to do. Ask yourself why you would want to harm yourself in this way? Correct your thinking in these moments of illogical thinking.
7. Notice the physical pain you feel when trying to match the facial expressions of others. Notice it in your face, your scalp and any other parts of your body when you are absorbed in anticipating what others are thinking or doing. Why are you doing that?

8. Learn that collectivists and moral dualists – most people on earth – are inept and poor judges of character. Their moral self-righteousness is wrong, misplaced and inappropriate to reality because they assume that you are part of a cosmic struggle against what they deem to be "the good."
9. Be fact-based in your relationship to reality and others. Contrary to the propagandists of religion, this is not a bad or cruel thing to do but the most humane thing of all.
10.　　Discover your base fears, tensions and pains. Learn to relate these to your subconscious thoughts and try to make them conscious. Once conscious they can be corrected by pursuing new knowledge.
11.　　Forgive. This may seem strange but the worst thing you can do is to build up anger against others. Release that anger by recognizing that pent-up anger is a result of the acts of cruelty imposed on you by those closest to you. Most of these people are struggling with the confusions imposed upon them by culture.

Conclusion

The Battle of the Sexes is a primitive religion. Christianity, now the dominant religion, has proscribed pleasure and sex to the point where people find it hard to believe that sex and illicit affairs could be part of any religion. In the past, before the dominance of Christian and Muslim religions, sex and sexual issues were not as taboo as they are today.

The Battle of the Sexes was originally a myth that became an established religion whose rituals were reenacted during its rites. In fact, if one looks closely into Christianity, one will find hints of this battle in the New Testament in the views that Christians hold toward women. To early Christians, women were to be avoided, ostracized, put in their place and muffled. They were considered unclean, seductive and sexually dangerous. This is a residue from religious views that saw all women as a form of Eve who was herself a form of Aphrodite, a woman who used her charms to seduce man and drive him out of Paradise.

Indeed, if you study the Middle Ages, that were dominated by Christianity, you find attitudes toward women to be oppressive and fearful. Women could be loving mothers but as "vixens" they were sometimes persecuted to death.

You even find this view especially among men today who practice the Muslim faith. All such views are a reaction to the more "liberated" views of women practiced in ancient times. This is because the Battle of the Sexes cult was an established religion at one time.

One can even say that the Christian religion is also a reaction to the view that man is like Ares, warlike, self-concerned and oppressive. In effect, Christianity, if it is anything, is an effort to make all men into Hephaistos, into a docile, impotent creature who is subservient to the Caesars (Ares) who conquered, ruled and portrayed themselves as foundational gods.

How does an individual become trapped within the roles of the battle of the sexes? It is one of the more interesting psychological concepts I've developed but, in my view, the prejudices found in the roles established by the Battle of the Sexes religion are passed from individual to individual by means of example. Each prejudice is passed generationally by means of the established religions of each generation; and since each religion had its own specific reaction to the original myth, this reaction is reflected in the attitudes of priests and parents and this is passed to the individual.

Each individual assumes that the prejudices regarding others' treatment of him are correct and then takes on the role exemplified by these prejudices. For instance, if everyone in his family and neighborhood treats the individual as if he were Hephaistos, let's say, bumbling, idiotic, incompetent and not worth taking seriously, despite the fact that those characteristics were not inherent in the individual, he will, in most cases, assume the role as his own personality and act as if it were true. He is now trapped in a culturally induced paradigmatic role; grist for the mill, so to speak.

By distorting roles among individuals, the Battle of the Sexes role paradigms distort motives, wishes, hopes and dreams. Because human relations are based upon roles steeped in prejudice, the result is corruption and false understandings among people. Suppressed energies and natures, poorly focused and irrationally conceived, create actions and goals that mean a violation of integrity for the individual.

When the paradigms one deals with in other people are themselves violations of the individual's right to self-create; when they distort the individual's understanding of himself they corrupt and distort value. Cynicism and chauvinism are the order of the day. We are left, unfortunately, with the world as it is.

Does the Battle of the Sexes paradigm sound familiar? As I mentioned before, it is the subject of hundreds of stories, novels and movies. The dances and ballets we watch of two lovers seducing each other are a reenactment of the Greek love story; the facial expressions of actors and real people with seductive smiles, flashing eyes, 'come hither' body language are all copied from the gods; they are emulations. They take place in bars and discos every night. Over and over, we read about, watch and participate in this story; over and over and many of us repeat the same rituals, the same reenactments in our own lives. "Your place or mine?" is the question asked by Ares. We are obedient "livers" of the lives of the gods, "lovers" doing what they did as they did –

just like our religious leaders of the past instructed us. This fact is a clue to the notion that there was once a religious rite that honored these gods and their "doings".

Despite the ritual, the humor, the sex and the laughing gods, I submit that there is a devastating effect for people "acting out" the assigned roles of the Battle of the Sexes religion. The psychological complexes they create literally destroy the ability of individuals to make sexual and romantic love decisions because of the false personal characteristics they take on. These roles interfere with those decisions by setting up emotional psychological blocks that make rational decisions impossible.

The only option for any of the roles within the Battle of the Sexes paradigm is to stiffen, deny one's fear of others, and attempt to overcome humiliation by transforming oneself into a muscular "action machine" that is always consumed by one goal – to reclaim lost love and enslave the love object; to overcome the consequences of the actions that have brought us to the dangerous precipice between almost losing love and having lost it. It is more important for this role to re-conquer by becoming its own antithesis. Love is secondary in the ritual known as the Battle of the Sexes. Only sex matters.

Why do so many people dutifully play the roles of the disenfranchised and cheated lover, the conquering hero or the beautiful and fickle female lover? They do this because they must, and they must because not to do so would anger the gods. Today it is not the anger of the gods we must fear but the anger of society. To live as the gods lived makes individuals good, makes them members of humanity, joiners of the collective, just like everyone else – and through this ritual, religion imparts value to people, by means of a reversal of cause and consequence – do this and you are good, let others watch you do this and you join humanity, you are an actor in the mystery of life, the battle for love.

But more than this, the stories are their own release. By ritually reenacting the myths of the gods in their own lives, people express and release negative energy that comes from the deep distress caused by social anxiety. Indeed, the very purpose of the early mystery religions and their rites was to facilitate catharsis, release and understanding of deep mysteries. The mystery rites were the precursors of our novels and movies. The scene in the Odyssey where the love story is told and danced was an early form of theater. It made people cry because they related to it in their own lives.

No human being can possibly possess personality characteristics that are imposed from the outside by others. For instance, only a sheer accident of nature could make a person a natural cuckold. This means that the individual who has been treated as a cuckold by others, through the influence of the Battle of the Sexes religion, never learns about his own characteristics, his own true complexity. This includes characteristics and capabilities that are built into the human system such as the ability to reason and to define values consciously – he seldom develops these capabilities because of the role he/she is playing. A struggle develops between anxiety and desire. He is a disintegrated mess.

The individual who is caught in a role trap is not able to relate to the individual that he *is*. That man is a creature with the capacity of reason is lost somewhere beneath these roles. That he is not allowed to discover reason ensures that he will come to think that playing a role is his only way of dealing with the world. That he is not allowed to discover reason ensures that he will never discover his true self.

This ambivalence, this confusion about the gods being like men and men being like the gods is a crucial juncture for man historically and psychologically because it originates primarily out of the relationship of a person with his family and peers. The psychological concept called incorporation takes place when the young individual "becomes" the characteristics of his parents. If his parents are deeply involved in reliving the story of the Battle of the Sexes in their own lives, they will exert influence on the younger individual that incorporates these roles into his own premises as they are implied in the parents' actions and attitudes. If his father is Mars-like or Hephaistos-like or even Aphrodite-like, he will see this role example as an option for himself. The same influence is exerted by the mother in her role acceptance. The younger individual merely sees, learns, imitates and treats people from within the rules of the paradigm, treating women like Aphrodite, men like Mars or Hephaistos, giving others in his life the additional anxiety of being constantly misunderstood and mistreated.

Of course a young person needs to learn how to accept his or her vulnerability when it comes to the capricious nature of some people in his life, but he need not accept the premises and roles of the Battle of the Sexes religion. He can reject those premises as full of delusions and prejudices and move away from them by a thorough analysis of how he has been led astray.

The solution is individualism and its creator reason.

About Robert Villegas

Robert Villegas is an Arizona author specializing in fiction, romance, theater and philosophy and religion. He was born in South Texas (Weslaco) but raised in Indiana. He is Hispanic-American but American in every sense of the word. He has spent a lifetime in the business world as a UPS executive and also worked in locations all over the United States and Europe. He is an Army veteran who served in Korea as a telecommunications specialist serving in the 7th Infantry Division in Camp Casey, Korea. He was educated in Indiana and earned a Degree through the University of the State of NY (Albany) via an external degree program. He is divorced with three grown children and three grandchildren.

These four books by Robert Villegas comprise some of the business books that he has written. As an executive working for several companies, he was able to develop these methods that will help anyone seeking to excel in the business world. These books are:

How to Be a Great Employee – and a Greater Manager

You cannot be a great manager without first being a great employee. And this is something that requires learning, experience and attitude. The attitude comes from you but the learning and experience you should acquire through diligent study and practice. http://amzn.to/2BqdG2i $3.99 Kindle $8.95 softcover

SWOT Analysis Supercharged

A SWOT Analysis is an objective look at the internal and external elements of your organization that impact your success or lack thereof. If done diligently, you will always have a handle on what you need to do to improve season after season. http://amzn.to/2BCAWYx $3.99 Kindle $6.95 softcover

The Five-Module Call Center Training System

The Five-Module Call Center Training System is designed to assist the Call Center Team Leader in helping his employees quickly upgrade their skills to an acceptable level. http://amzn.to/2B3Svj1 $3.99 Kindle $5.95 softcover

Website Development Methodology

Effective strategic marketing requires the ability to differentiate the website development organization and its deliverables from those of the competition. http://amzn.to/2DnYMqh $2.99 Kindle $12.95 softcover.

www.robertvillegas.com

Alcoholism and Addiction – the System

These four books comprise a system that can be used by both patients and counselors who are battling Alcoholism and Addiction. Based upon Mr. Villegas's own system developed during his struggle against alcoholism, this system includes:

Alcoholism and Addiction – A Secular Ten-Step Program

This groundbreaking book offers a secular approach to alcoholism unlike that offered by Alcoholics Anonymous. We recommend that every individual going for alcohol and drug-abuse counseling be given a copy of this book which contains the workbook and the two versions of The World's first drunk. http://amzn.to/2md6R9w $3.45 Kindle $11.95 softcover

The Secular Ten-Step Program Workbook

This booklet covers the program developed by Mr. Villegas. It is designed as a workbook with blank spaces for the patient to write his own thoughts as he takes each of the ten steps. Order one copy for each patient in counseling. http://amzn.to/2lrHimS $4.49 Kindle $6.95 softcover

The World's First Drunk – With Counselor Talking Points

This booklet is designed for the counselor as he works with patients during individual or group therapy. It contains helpful tips on discussing the life story of the man who invented alcohol. Order one copy for each patient in counseling. http://amzn.to/2l446Wr $2.99 Kindle $5.95 softcover

The World's First Drunk – Patient Version

This version of the short story contains empty spaces where the patient can answer questions about the life story of the man who invented alcohol. Order one copy for each counselor. http://amzn.to/2ldxBGb $2.99 Kindle $5.95 softcover.

www.robertvillegas.com

The Mark of Titus

Excerpts from the book Unkilling Jesus which highlight some of the key discoveries implied by new theories about the origin of the Jesus Myth. The idea that the Romans invented Christianity is the basic premise of new theories about the origin of Christianity.http://amzn.to/2itMCo0 $3.49 Kindle $5.95 softcover

Contra Religion

This book is designed as a "shorter" explanation of the ideas presented in my larger book, "Behind the Ritual Mask" which seeks to define fundamental principles of religion. I'm hoping this book will serve as a primer for the original book and spur an interest in reading it. http://amzn.to/2yWMSlx $3.99 Kindle $6.95 softcover

Is this the Face that Launched a Thousand Ships?

It was love at first sight. I saw her one day while watching a television program about King Tut, whose tomb had been discovered by Howard Carter years before. I was looking at the famous bust of a beautiful Egyptian Queen. https://amzn.to/3t487x3 $3.99 Kindle $7.95 softcover

The History of Altruism

The History of Altruism is a historical treatment of the development of altruism throughout time from the Paleolithic period to today. It tracks the development of self-sacrifice of primitive man to the advent of altruism as a development from Kant's "duty". It covers a broad sweep of concepts and shows how they influenced modern man, religion and societies through the ages. https://amzn.to/3gN8zgy $4.19 Kindle 14.95 paperback.

www.robertvillegas.com

Books on Christianity

Unkilling Jesus

Who was Paul and what was his role in the creation of Christianity? What was his provenance, and did he meet the resurrected Christ? Who wrote Revelation and what was the document's purpose? Why was Domitian assassinated? http://amzn.to/2itMCo0 $3.99 Kindle $15.95 softcover

Domitian: The Final Messiah

The central goal of this book is to define the specific themes and concepts that make up Domitian's contribution to Christianity – in a sense, we are defining the specific Domitian overlay to the Christian materials originally developed for Titus. http://amzn.to/2yWMSlx $2.99 Kindle $6.95 softcover

Paul's Agon and the Mystification of History

Paul and Jesus are joined in one important way; the way of a miracle. They met on the road to Damascus while Paul supposedly pursued Christians. Jesus, in a sense, told Paul to get with the program and stop persecuting his people. In this incident, the Bible tells us that Jesus is already dead, and resurrected. This book argues otherwise. http://amzn.to/2zSDsuP $5.99 Kindle $19.95 softcover

Christianity on the Arch of Titus

This book explores the "persons" visible on the Triumphant Arch of Titus which is located in the heart of Rome. These people were significant in that they played a role, not only in Rome's conquest of Judaea but also in the creation of Christianity. This book explores those individuals and the roles they played in the creation of one of the most important religious movements in world history. https://amzn.to/3xz3OgM $3.69 Kindle 10.95 paperback.

www.robertvillegas.com

The REAL Purpose-Driven Life

After centuries of being told that it is not about you, it is time to set the record straight. You are a unique individual and your goal in life should be to achieve your own happiness.
https://amzn.to/2XyrpPf $3.50 Kindle $7.95 softcover

Values and Purpose Workbook

This book is about you. It's about time. After centuries of being told that nothing is about you, it is time to set the record straight. You are a unique individual and your goal in life should be to achieve your happiness. https://amzn.to/2XwlkTv $3.99 Kindle $8.95 softcover

www.robertvillegas.com

Values and Purpose Books by Robert Villegas

The Real Purpose-Driven Life

After centuries of being told that it is not about you, it is time to set the record straight. You are a unique individual and your goal in life should be to achieve your own happiness. This book is about helping you accomplish your goals and fixing your purpose firmly in place. It covers not only why you should pursue your goals but how to do it. https://amzn.to/3ebkhjr $3.99 Kindle $6.95 softcover

The Values and Purpose Workbook

Rather than give you tasks that involve doing a lot of things for other people, I'm am going to tell you that focusing on yourself will reveal your life's purpose and express your passions and freedom. I'm going to start with you. https://amzn.to/3eQf4wG $2.99 Kindle $6.95 softcover

This Book is About You

Some people move briskly bent on a purpose, concerned only about what they are about. People walk by them; they don't even notice. They just keep to their path and you wonder where they are going. This book is about you. It's about time. https://amzn.to/3vFMzss $6299 Kindle $5.95 softcover

www.robertvillegas.com

Self-Help Books by Robert Villegas

Existence a Rational Thoughtbook

A Rational Thoughtbook is designed for thinking as opposed to reading. It combines brief prescient content with stunning imagery. Existence focuses on the nature of existence and gives you intelligent thoughts to integrate into your life.

https://amzn.to/2RZpsKV $4.99 Kindle $12.95 softcover

The Virtue of Independence

One of the most important goals for any person is to establish intellectual independence. Intellectual independence is the road to "life" independence, which is the ability to earn your own way without help from others. https://amzn.to/3awuCV2 $2.99 Kindle $6.95 softcover

Rational Meditation

Rational Meditation is self-meditation. It is thinking about yourself without guilt and without the tenets of modern philosophy (that the world is unknowable, that man is a phony, that ethics and living are only about others). https://amzn.to/3gus9OE $6.99 Kindle $12.95 softcover

History of My Mind

This booklet is the companion to my book entitled Rational Meditation. It utilizes the various exercises of the original book that involve contemplation or meditation and provide space for written input by the reader. https://amzn.to/3gy3hpl $4.69 Kindle $11.95 softcover.

www.robertvillegas.com

Fiction and Creative Poems and Plays

   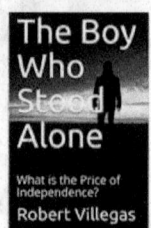

Poetic Prose and Poetry

These expressions represent some of Mr. Villegas' deepest thoughts as he lived and traveled throughout the world in locations such as Germany (East and West), Austria, Britain, Spain, Canada, France, Luxembourg, Belgium, the Netherlands, Korea, New York, Miami, San Francisco and other locations. https://amzn.to/3vu7X3B $2.99 Kindle $6.95 softcover

The Lost Poems

These poems were discovered among Mr. Villegas's archives in 2016. Many of them have been read by only Mr. Villegas. Most of these poems were rejected as "not that good". After seeing them again, he has changed his mind. These poems expressive, fresh and spontaneously honest. https://amzn.to/3aPg5nB $3.99 Kindle $6.95 softcover

Adam Reborn – A Short Play

Adam Reborn is a play of symbols. Adam and Eve, as I have portrayed them, are young and heroic people learning to deal with a Paradise and God that are hostile to them. There is no chance of life for them. https://amzn.to/3u9Nr8b $2.99 Kindle $6.95 softcover

The Boy Who Stood Alone

Jonny Payne has just discovered Ayn Rand and his parents don't know what to do. They take him to a priest and a psychologist but his only question is "What is the price of independence? https://amzn.to/3nCG6ve $3.99 Kindle $6.95 paperback.

www.robertvillegas.com

Fiction and Creative Materials

Aphrodite

Johnny is a Spanish guitar player with a mysterious past. At a party, he meets the beautiful songstress Aphrodite who is enthralled with his flamenco guitar skills. Later, she learns they have a connection, a particular song they both appear to know. Aphrodite discovers the connection, and through dreams, the two fall in love. The question is whether they will ever be together. https://amzn.to/3xIlmXZ $3.99 Kindle $5.95 softcover

The Odyssey of Amerigo the Founder

Amerigo was born in a time of desperation and dystopia. He was the only man with the vision of a great future. Many repaired to his cause while others swore to destroy him. They wanted his life, his mind and everything he loved. He swore that no matter what they did, he would win the struggle for freedom and a new future. https://amzn.to/2Qz8h2t $3.99 Kindle $8.95 softcover

Bob and Bobbie

1967 - a town outside Camp Casey, Korea - two young people have come together to challenge a world that makes love impossible. https://amzn.to/3sZWSpf $2.99 Kindle $5.95 softcover

The Raven Haired Girl

Bobby met Angie 52 years ago in a poor neighborhood in Indianapolis. It was love at first sight. For a few short months, their relationship blossomed into love. They were in love but didn't know how to be in love because they were only fourteen years old. https://amzn.to/3306plF $2.99 Kindle $6.95 paperback.

www.robertvillegas.com

Poems for the Stage

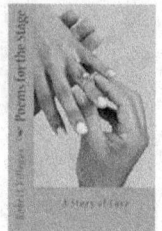 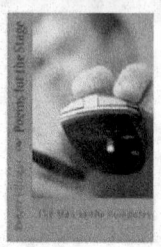

Poems for the Stage – A Story of Love

This dramatic presentation features poems found in Mr. Villegas's book Poetic Prose and Poetry. Some are also found in his book.
https://amzn.to/3gSJctV $2.99 Kindle $5.95 softcover

Poems for the Stage – The Man at the Computer

This dramatic presentation is based upon poems from Mr. Villegas's book Poetic Prose and Poetry. Some of the poems have been slightly altered to reflect the internal story. Mr. Villegas's book Poetic Prose and Poetry can be found on Amazon.com.
https://amzn.to/2R8zpFf $2.99 Kindle $5.95 softcover

www.robertvillegas.com

A Boomer takes on the Far Left

I just learned something about myself – and it isn't very good. In fact, it is very bad. I learned that the opinions of Boomers don't matter any more. We are obsolete in this new age of new knowledge. Anything we think is unimportant and false. I don't think so. https://amzn.to/3tzNqtc $5.19 Kindle $10.95 softcover

Crushing the Alinsky Radicals

The worst enemy of individual rights today is a group of people I call the Alinsky Radicals. These people are now in charge of our culture and temporarily, in charge of government. They are associated, philosophically and politically, with the communists and fascists of the past. They are not your father's liberals. They are the direct descendants of dictators such as Stalin and Mao. In this book, I hope to convince you of the evil of the Alinsky Radicals and to provide the intellectual ammunition you need to eradicate them from society. https://amzn.to/3hbh9WN $3.49 Kindle $8.95 softcover

The Conservative's Dilemma

I wrote this book to ask some important questions about the conservative philosophy of altruism. https://amzn.to/3bfDQ8e $2.99 Kinde $6.95 softcover.

The Biggest Mistakes in History – 2008 to 2016

To be the Chief Executive of the greatest country in the world requires a leader with a great deal of knowledge, experience and reasoning ability. It requires having the very best minds as advisors, minds that the President can count on to give reasoned arguments and detailed knowledge about the important issues of the day. I think it takes a special ability to understand the principle of cause and effect concerning how government action impacts the lives of real people. https://amzn.to/3tDQ4Ol $2.99 Kindle $10.95 softcover

www.robertvillegas.com

Dachau and Berlin in 1990

This booklet chronicles Mr. Villegas' thoughts during visits to Dachau and Berlin during 1990, disclosing my observations of milestones in German history, past and present, and relating those events to world happenings as they were unfolding at the time. I traveled throughout Germany for much of 1990 while on business. https://amzn.to/3ex578d $2.99 Kindle $6.95 softcover

What Harvard and Princeton Don't Want You to Know

The professors at Harvard and Princeton don't want you to know about the worst ideas in history. This is because they have been pawning these ideas off as true and profound. They have been using them to deceive and manipulate us for centuries. https://amzn.to/3farP5p $5.19 Kindle $9.95 softcover

Defending American Values

This book is made up of several chapters about American values and how they can be defended without a descent into the abyss of dictatorship. The book argues for individual rights and provides reasons why we should fight for them. https://amzn.to/3uMFq9L $3.99 Kinde $5.95 softcover.

Capitalism Doesn't Fail

How many times have we heard the old saw: "Capitalism has failed again" over the course of contemporary events? We heard it during the Great Depression of 1929 after Hoover had invoked tariffs and precipitated economic retaliation and a banking crisis. Along with this question usually came a statement to the effect, that "We can fix capitalism and make it even stronger by issuing economic controls or spending money to stimulate economic activity." This book will argue that capitalism, as an economic system, cannot fail as long as individuals are free to act. https://amzn.to/3xZIAJ6 $4.19 Kindle $10.95 softcover

www.robertvillegas.com

Finding Sponsors 1 and 2

This book is written for anyone seeking sponsorship relationships in the sport and entertainment fields. The ideas and principles presented here are applicable to any company, sport team, entertainment company, marketing agency and charitable organization that uses corporate sponsorships to support its activities. Volume 1: https://amzn.to/3ejm1Hp $5.19 Kindle $12.95 softcover Volume 2: https://amzn.to/3eVDo0e $4.69 Kindle $10.95 softcover

How to Write a Sponsorship Proposal

This booklet provide you with some basic guidelines on what to communicate in order to produce a winning sponsorship proposal. These guidelines will focus on what you should be presenting to your potential sponsor to make the best business case for involvement with your team or entertainment company. $2.99 Kindle $6.95 softcover

Hospitality Event Planning Handbook

One key part of your sponsorship activation strategy might be customer hospitality events in conjunction with sporting events. How do you pull off a Hospitality Event for your biggest customers? You may not know how to start, what to do and how to ensure the event is a success. This book can help. http://amzn.to/2mxzpgy $7.95 softcover.

Selling Sponsorship in the Age of the Coronavirus

This book provides suggestions on how sport teams, athletes and concert promoters can mitigate the damage done to their businesses by the economic lockdowns (due to the Coronavirus). It integrates checklists, SWOT Analysis and other valuable business aids into one toolkit that will help you keep your sport and/or genre alive in these difficult times. https://amzn.to/2QVBNiM $5.15 Kindle $5.95 softcover

www.robertvillegas.com